The World of Emily Howland
Odyssey of a Humanitarian

D1603129

Emily Howland

The World of Emily Howland

Odyssey of a Humanitarian

Judith Colucci Breault

LES FEMMES
Millbrae, California

Copyright © 1976, 1974 by Judith Colucci Breault

LES FEMMES
231 Adrian Road
Millbrae, California 94030

First Printing, January 1976
Made in the United States of America

Library of Congress Cataloging in Publication Data

Breault, Judith Colucci, 1946–
    The world of Emily Howland.

    Bibliography: p.
    Includes index.
    1. Howland, Emily, 1827–1929.   2. United States
—Social conditions—To 1865.   3. United States—
Social conditions—1865–1918.   I.   Title.
HQ1413.H68B73   301.24'20924   [B]   75-10580
ISBN 0-89087-987-7
ISBN 0-89087-904-4 pbk.

1 2 3 4 5 − 79 78 77 76

For George

Preface

While tentatively investigating the world of women's experiences in nineteenth century America, I met one of those rare historical figures a researcher can only hope to encounter once in a lifetime. She was Emily Howland, a woman whose tumultuous 101-year life extended from America's early national period through to the end of the Jazz Age. Born in 1827, Emily was the quiet, introspective, only daughter of a prosperous rural New York Quaker family. As she matured Emily became a complex, sensitive woman deeply immersed in social reform and agitation. She threw her considerable energy, time and efforts into the budding antislavery and woman's rights movements in the 1840s and '50s, initiated her own radical interracial project in the South during Reconstruction and then became intensely committed to peace and temperance reform as well as to the education of blacks and women. Like so many of her fellow female reformers, Emily remained caring, concerned and committed to social activism until the time of her death in 1929.

But Emily Howland was more than just an active figure in a broad segment of key nineteenth century movements and reforms. Warm, articulate and introspective, Emily was also a skilled writer who perceptively chronicled the growth taking place within her own life as well as in American society. Emily managed to capture the pace and sense of American social change over time while exploring the details of her own odyssey first as daughter, then as woman, and finally as venerated sage. Her daily routines, intimate female friendships, family ties, Friendly communities, and revealing fantasies together formed the boundaries of her world and defined the direction and scope of her 101-year odyssey.

The changing cast of characters accompanying Emily on this journey includes names which should be, but unfortunately are not, familiar to us today. The world of Emily Howland did exist in nineteenth century America yet both Emily and her group of friends, family and reformers have fallen victim to a limited historical vision. We are just now beginning to recognize that women have been sorely neglected in the literature of American social reform and that their daily experiences in the past three centuries have been similarly overlooked. Women and their political, social and economic roles have been and still are victims of the traditional historian's silence, making our understanding of the history of America, in fact, an understanding of the history of American men.

This book is one attempt in helping us regain a sense of our past. As we read about Emily's unique odyssey as a woman, we may begin to understand ourselves better and the significance of these historical roots in our lives today and for the future.

Cast of Characters

Family

Slocum Howland .... Emily's parents
Hannah Tallcot Howland
William Howland .... Emily's brothers
Benjamin Howland
Hannah Letchworth Howland .... Emily's sister-in-law
Isabel Howland .... Emily's niece
Susan Baker .... Emily's "adopted" daughter

Personal Friends

✯Susanna Marriott.................. Abolitionist/teacher/Quaker
Anna Searing .... Teacher/neighbor/Quaker
Emma Brown .... Teaching Assistant/Non-Quaker
Ellen Child .... Philadelphia Quaker
Gulie Jones .... Philadelphia Quaker
Katie Mulhall...................... New York protegee/Doctor
Charles W. Folsom............. Boston abolitionist/Non-Quaker
James Ferree .... New York abolitionist/Non-Quaker
Edward Strange................ English ex-convict/Non-Quaker

Reformers

✹ Mary Grew .... Philadelphia abolitionist/feminist/Non-Quaker
✹ Margaret Jones Burleigh. Philadelphia abolitionist/feminist/Quaker
Cornelia Hancock ...... Civil War nurse/feminist/teacher/Quaker
✯ Sallie Holley .... New York abolitionist/feminist/Non-Quaker
✶ Myrtilla Miner ...... New York abolitionist/educator/Non-Quaker
Mary Reed .... Philadelphia teacher/Non-Quaker
Mary Robinson .... Philadelphia teacher/Non-Quaker
Anna Howard Shaw................ Minister/lecturer/suffragist
Susan B. Anthony .... New York feminist leader/Quaker
Elizabeth Cady Stanton..... New York feminist leader/Non-Quaker

Acknowledgments

Among the research librarians who assisted me in this biographical study, I owe a special note of thanks to Jane Rittenhouse, Eleanor Maier and Nancy Spears of the Friends Historical Library, Swarthmore, PA, and to Nancy Dean of the Manuscript Division of the John Olin Library, Cornell University.

Thanks are also due to Phebe M. King of Scipio Center, N.Y., for her kindness, help and encouragement; to Margaret Hope Bacon, Carroll Smith-Rosenberg, John Caughey, Michael Zuckerman and Robert Zemsky for their reading of the manuscript at various stages in its evolution from dissertation to book; and to George Breault for his patience and loving support.

Contents

Illustrations

PART I

*Introduction to
The World of Emily Howland*

Introduction

The signs had become unmistakable in the year 1857, even here in the little village of Sherwood, New York, that the North was beginning, at long last to unite in its opposition to slavery. Since March 6th when the United States Supreme Court had announced its decision on the Dred Scott case, denying the rights of slaves to standing as citizens, the major tone of the Northern response was becoming increasingly fiery as well as moral. Slavery was being viewed as a danger to Christian and American principles of democracy and constitutional government. It was enough to gladden the heart of any abolitionist and the decidedly Quaker town of Sherwood had its share.

There was nothing visibly distinctive about the town which would distinguish it from any of the other small towns perched similarly on the ridges surrounding the Finger Lakes in central New York State. Interchangeably known as Sherwood or Sherwood's Corners, the village, in existence for a little over a half century, was nearing its peak of growth. In the mid-1790s a handful of families from New England, Judge Seth Sherwood among them, had stopped on this spot on the Poplar Ridge and built frame houses around the crossroads. In 1804 Sherwood was selected as the county seat but the honor was shortlived—the designation was revoked the following year.

During this time a small number of Quaker families, like so many other families around the turn of the nineteenth century, had moved across New York State from New England in search of richer farming lands and pastures. As the Quaker families arrived in Sherwood, their actions were similar to those of others settling in this new land. The men built their frame houses and meeting places for worship and business, cleared land, jointly constructed barns and sheds, sowed seed and raised animals; the women bore and raised children and performed those heavy domestic duties that were considered their lot. By 1820 many of the original non-Quakers, including all of the Sherwoods, had moved farther west, leaving only the Sherwood name at the crossroads as evidence of their short stay in this region. On the other hand, the small band of Quakers continued to expand in number, benefiting from the influx of fellow Friends arriving each year in modest numbers.

Now in 1857 Sherwood continued to have a distinctively rural Quaker appearance with four local meeting houses standing in testi-

1

mony to the strength of the village's Quaker heritage. Many of the Friends in Sherwood found their economic livelihood firmly bound to the fertile land surrounding the village. That summer the future of their crops held the same important place in their thoughts as it had in previous summers. In late July as evening approached, one can imagine the farmers sitting inside Slocum Howland's general supply store. While the lightning flashed and the rain beat down, the conversation might have revolved around the hailstorm and widespread flooding that had swept through the area earlier that month damaging crops.

An uncomplicated bucolic scene should not be drawn from this conjecture for these men of Sherwood were not the stereotype of the simple yeoman farmer. Most were literate, many widely read. Among them were teachers, preachers, abolitionists and prohibitionists as knowledgeable about events in the world outside Sherwood as they were about the newest agricultural methods used on their crops.

Slocum Howland was such a man. Tall and thin, kindly and gentle, with a shock of graying hair and piercing eyes, he played an important role in the community beyond that of storekeeper. A devout member of the Society of Friends, he carried the Quaker ethic of fairness, honesty and shrewdness into his business dealings with friends and neighbors. By the mid-1850s he had become an informal banking institution for the community, extending credit, establishing mortgages, lending money and trading stock. A grain speculator, manufacturer and contractor, with his economic future resting in the world outside as well as within, Howland followed the national and state economic fluctuations with an avid interest that was rivaled only by his commitment to abolitionism. Howland's house was a station on the Underground Railroad; the *Liberator, Philanthropist* and *National Anti-Slavery Standard* were fixtures in the home. Slocum also made contributions regularly to state and national abolitionist organizations. Each spring the community would know when the American Anti-Slavery Convention was to be held for Slocum Howland would close his store for four consecutive days to attend the annual meeting.

He became an abolitionist out of a deliberate rational commitment to certain ethical values, Quaker in form and content. Like many of his fellow Friends and neighbors, Slocum believed that "all

Emily Howland, her father Slocum Howland and the family dog Grant in the 1870s. (Courtesy Friends Historical Library of Swarthmore College)

mankind was of one blood." He stood firm in the face of opposition, scorn and contempt, feeling that these views should be upheld "with immovable firmness."

Slocum equated his abolitionism with William Lloyd Garrison and no other. He believed that Garrison, like the prophets of old, was raised up by the Almighty to lead a holy crusade to rid the nation of the sin of slavery. He argued that human bondage was intolerable in a democratic society and fearless people were needed to take an uncompromising stand against the tyranny of the slavocracy.

Since the Dred Scott Decision which had enflamed the sectional slavery controversy between North and South, Slocum no longer had to look only to fellow Garrisonians to find those who were now willing to defy the dictates of the Supreme Court. But if this picture of increasing abolitionist sentiment temporarily brightened Slocum's outlook, his personal sense of optimism was to be short-lived. As spring stretched into summer, the economic panic and its subsequent recession ended an intense period of speculation and prosperity. Although agricultural Sherwood was relatively immune from the worst effects of this industrial disturbance, Slocum Howland did suffer what later proved to be temporary economic setbacks.

On July 29, in the midst of these social and economic dislocations, a small interruption in the quiet flow of daily life in Sherwood occurred. Emily Howland, the twenty-nine year old unmarried daughter of Slocum and Hannah Howland, left Sherwood by stagecoach to visit with friends in neighboring Auburn. This certainly had the appearance of a most ordinary event and few would have recognized it for what it was to become: the first tentative steps in an odyssey that was to last seventy-two years. When Emily Howland arrived at her friend's home in Auburn later that day, she penned this not so ordinary letter to her mother Hannah:

> Dear Mother:
> Now I am going to write upon the matter in my thoughts because it is easier to write than to talk of it. I have forborne to mention it, because it was all uncertainty, and knowing it was a painful subject I would not needlessly bring it up.
> It is. May I give a little of my life to degraded humanity? May I work a little while for that class which has so long enlisted my closest sympathies? May I try if I really can to make the world a little better for having lived in it? Can't thee spare me a while to do what I think my portion? I want to do something which seems to me worthy of life, and if all my life is to go on as have the last ten years, I know I shall feel at the end of it

as tho' I had lived in vain, others with perhaps not as much capacity had reared noble, worthy families, contributed their share to the world and I had done nothing, dwindled away. I know thy health is very poor but I can do nothing for it, and as long as no one would think of its deterring me from marrying and leaving home forever if I choose, (Most think very strange that I do not, doubtless) it certainly can no more be urged against my taking a few years or months perhaps, for a benevolent enterprise.

Thee may think other daughters remain at home contentedly why can't I? Because I have inherited such an amount of the desire to work that I cannot. If I am different from the stereotyped kind I can't help it. I must be filled. For the last thirteen years I have been busy about nothing, it did not satisfy me, it never can, until I have done something more.

With the most despised and forlorn, my heart is, let me go to them and see what good I can do them.

Do not ask any one but thy own self whether to let Emily go or not. It is not a question of propriety, I have allowed my ideas of duty often to be crushed by such counsel, nothing, no good thought or work was ever given to the world that did not look queer to the most of folks. I have the consolation of being approved in the plan by those who know me best. It has been a darling plan of mine for years, to do something for the outcast race whose destiny involves such great results—the hopes of this country—now the opportunity is mine, such a one may not come again. Let me improve it!

Farewell affectionately,
Emily

Hardly a letter written by a woman "by nature timid, shrinking and illy calculated to cope with the mammon of unrighteousness!" as Emily had recently called herself. More extraordinary, it was written by a twenty-nine year old daughter to her mother seeking permission to chart a course in a world totally unfamiliar to either of them.

Who was this daughter who considered herself far "different from the stereotyped kind?" Emily Howland was already a study in contrasts and contradictions to her family and friends in Sherwood. Physically, she was small like her mother Hannah. She shared with her father Slocum those dark intense eyes, a penetrating gaze, and the burning desire to help her fellow humans. Yet there was no severity or harshness in Emily's face or bearing. She gave the overwhelming impression of being a warm, open and decidely pleasant person.

Yet, here she was, a woman on the far edge of youth, who wished to go to the "despised and forlorn," to enter into a radical activity alien to all experience previously encountered in the rural ebb and flow of life in Sherwood. Emily wanted to leave the comfort and security of her home and family to teach in the controversial Miner School for free black girls in Washington, D.C. Myrtilla Miner was ill and a new director was needed if the school was to continue into the next term. Emily would be isolated in a schoolhouse on the outskirts of the city, in a hostile environment, with only a few friends in the nearby Capital willing to help her adjust to her new life.

Emily obviously had thought fully about this venture and recognized the advantages as well as the disadvantages to such a plan. Although in this letter Emily appears to be asking for Hannah's permission to embark on this new venture, she was already ensured of receiving her mother's consent. Emily had carefully anticipated and countered all possible arguments against her going long before Hannah could raise them. Much lay beyond the words in this letter. A number of events had precipitated Emily's unusual request, but to understand Emily and her actions requires more than a casual backward glance into the past. Emily Howland may have placed her foot on the path to Washington that summer day but the first steps were taken many years earlier.

1

Tentative Steps

In the village of Sherwood on November 20, 1827, the second, and only female, child of Slocum and Hannah Howland was born and named Emily. The family raised Emily and her two brothers, William and Benjamin, in a house adjacent to Slocum's store west of the crossroads. Her maternal and paternal grandparents lived within three miles of Sherwood during much of Emily's youth.

In years to come Emily was to reflect that in "Looking back to childhood, I see, as chief among those who inspired my inner life, or swayed my actions, my father, my grandfather and the teacher under whose care I was placed when about nine years old." Slocum in his relationship with his only daughter believed in what Emily termed a "wholesome letting alone." He seldom disciplined, commended or advised, believing that a large measure of freedom was necessary for Emily's proper development.

On the other hand, Emily's devout maternal grandfather, Joseph Tallcot, set rigid expectations for Emily, requiring her to follow carefully all the rules of the Quaker sect. The two most important men during Emily's childhood held diametrically opposing views about raising children, which may have caused Emily some confusion in her relationships with them and other adults in her family. But if Emily felt herself caught in any crosscurrents of conflicting childrearing practices, she never spoke of it. Instead, she remembered fondly how Joseph Tallcot spent many hours with her during her early childhood, teaching her to read and recite the New Testament, and guiding her to attain "the strictest uprightness of character."

From the time Emily was weaned, her mother had been sending her to live for increasingly large portions of time in the homes of her maternal relatives. More often than not, Emily spent extended visits with her Aunt Phebe in Skaneateles, New York, a half-day journey from Sherwood's Corners. On one such occasion, Emily's mother Hannah wrote to her sister Phebe saying: "How thankful I feel that thee keep Emily and improve her, my family so takes my attention that it is impossible to do by her as I should wish."

Hannah may have occupied a significant place in Emily's early life, providing the maternal nurturance and succor vital and necessary to a young child. Emily however consciously omitted maternal references when later speaking of her early childhood.

One of Hannah Howland's greatest interests was education and by the age of eight, Emily had made the move to a Friends' boarding school in neighboring Venice to begin her formal education. She wrote few letters during that year but those she penned were to her mother. The messages were suprisingly similar:

> O dear mother most of the little girls has the pleasure of seeing their parents on meeting day but I cannot see thee only when I go home; I often think I had rather be at home but I see the advantages arising from a good education which makes me more contented. We have been so very busily employed that we have not had time to play for several intermissions.

In the words "meeting day" rests the key to Hannah Howland's relations with those around her. Strict in her observance of the doctrines of George Fox, as were her parents before her, Hannah was a quiet and pious member of the Orthodox Quaker meeting, using plain dress and language at all times. Hannah preferred to spend her day of worship at the red brick meeting house west of Sherwood rather than with her daughter at the school in Venice. To Hannah it apparently seemed to be the spiritually correct thing to do. When Emily remembered other female members of her extended family, it was primarily in relation to the restrictions and customs of the Society of Friends. In an interview at age one hundred, Emily's memories of early childhood centered on the Society's adherence to plain dress. "I shall never forget my first picnic. After much pleading I was allowed to go. Little Quaker that I was, my skirts were long, to my ankles and below. It was just the day of short skirts and the long pantalets. I was the only girl at the picnic without them. And I was indeed unhappy. It was a long time before I would go to another."

After Emily's death in 1929, carefully folded in the attic of her home, a somber checked silk frock for a little girl was found. Ankle length, plainly made, Princess style, it bore this inscription written in Emily's hand:

> This is my dress when I was six or seven years old. I never had a short dress as Friends thought they were not plain. Aunt Sarah Merritt took me in hand once after meeting and told me the dress was too gay for a little Friend. She said not to wear it any more—to tell mother I did not want to wear it. After that I was afraid to wear it.

Slowly a picture begins to emerge of a small intense child being raised somberly if somewhat confusedly, with Quaker principles. Some relief from the austere childrearing practices of the Tallcots contrasted with the permissive tactics of Slocum Howland occurs when Emily, at the age of ten entered Susanna Marriott's boarding school in Aurora, four miles distant from Sherwood on the shores of Lake Cayuga. Although the Orthodox Quaker training continued with its strict adherence to plain garb and speech, Emily was introduced to new dimensions in the Quaker testimonies and experience through the warmth and vitality of Susanna Marriott.

Emily saw herself as a child whose "early training fostered intensity in a naturally quiet nature, and a little girl who played too little and who thought too much and suffered from headaches;" She "graduated from her grandfather's knee into a school for little girls." In sharp contrast to Slocum Howland, Susanna Marriott commended as heartily as she reproved, using a sense of discipline that was stern but just. Emily liked to compare her to Margaret Fuller, feeling that both possessed androgynous qualities. Marriott's most notable characteristics, in Emily's view, were similar to those designations given to Fuller: "a large-brained woman and large-hearted man."

The little girl of quiet thoughtful ways admired her teacher, Susanna Marriott, more than any woman in the community. The first fancy needlework that Emily attempted, filling in with worsted a small square of canvas, was under the direction of, as Emily referred to her, "that venerable English lady." What amused the young girl in this introduction to the feminine arts was the nature of the article upon which she was working. Bearing the legend "Anti-slave-holder," this double punned potholder was to be sold at the community fair with proceeds going to the local antislavery society.

Like Emily's father, Susanna Marriott collected antislavery books and those, with the main Garrisonian journals, constituted a loan library for the use of the community. Even more of an activist than Slocum Howland, she also brought lecturers from Boston, singly and in groups, once or twice a year, to keep interest in the cause alive. She organized benefits and community fairs, and circulated petitions for the abolition of slavery in the District of Columbia. In all these ways, Marriott was trying to teach Emily to recognize "the voice of God speaking to the soul of man," to bear witness for what she felt was right. Throughout this period the picture remains that of a solitary child immersed in concerns beyond her years. Emily herself tells us:

> In the dawn of my reading days the *Anti-Slavery Standard* entered our house. It has colored all the texture of thought and principle and swayed the course of my life more than any other influence; it has been 'the University' for me. Surely no paper can be to me what this has been; the love of my youth, the inspiration and the culture of mature years, worthy of immortal classic fame.

Many afternoons, first at home and then at Marriott's, were passed reading primers, in prose and verse, telling "tales of slavery, pathetic accounts of escapes from bondage, or sometimes of little colored boys and girls stolen from their homes and sold for slaves." Emily's favorite when very young was the monthly publication *The Slaves Friend.* The cover bore a picture of two little girls, one white and one black, playing among flowers, teaching that children of a darker hue should enjoy an equal share of the pleasures of life. Emily took the lesson to heart and made a practical application of it when the black woman who came to wash for the Howlands, brought her little girl, about Emily's age. Taking her by the hand, Emily led her into her father's store where Emily notes: "I received the raillery

of the clerk, which I felt proud to bear with the spirit of a martyr."
Emily obviously received support and encouragement for such behavior and for her antislavery reading from both her family and
Susanna Marriott. For Emily, antislavery may have been a very
important means of gaining approval from the four vastly different
people surrounding her during childhood.

In this manner, with the antislavery cause as a central focus, the
next four years at school and home passed swiftly as Susanna
Marriott with her fine literary tastes and strong social conscience,
directed Emily's intellectual and moral training. The twice daily
religious services and the reading of abolitionist sentiments did not
encompass all that Susanna offered her students. Her fondness of
poetry and her love for flowers fanned a similar spark within Emily
that flamed for the rest of her life.

During these years, when the number of zealous abolitionist
speakers increased in frequency in Cayuga County, Emily, although
young, began to attend their conventions in the meeting house and
homes of the local antislavery people. Emily was then able to listen
to their conversations around the dinner table and in the parlors.
Emily felt, at these times, as though she was in the presence of intelligent people dedicated to reforming a society of which she had little
knowledge. Her perceptions of the world outside of Sherwood were
slowly being shaped and colored by the words of these abolitionists.
Approaching puberty, Emily's vision had begun to extend beyond
the confines of the village and the sect.

Emily found the early 1840s a time of abrupt yet satisfying
change. She left Susanna Marriott's to attend the Poplar Ridge
Seminary in the home of Friend Wanzer, where she "enjoyed the
freedom never known before" in these "red letter days in the calendar of my youth. For the first time in my life I felt free and exhila-
rated." This freedom and exhilaration took many forms, the most
notable being political and moral in tone. In 1844, when only seventeen years old, Emily and three female classmates wrote and signed
an open petition to the Whigs of the community. The appeal began
with a declaration by the females that it was not their pleasure but
their *duty* to offer their aid and influence so that the wavering individual would espouse their cause in the upcoming presidential
election. Advising the Whigs to let "No Texas" be their motto, they
appealed dramatically to the men's humanity, to "stop the cursed

step of slavery, persevere till every bond is broken, and the clanking of no chain is heard within our borders; let your sympathies be aroused, your better feelings animated into action and your whole heart engaged in the cause of liberty to prevent the extension of this evil. It will be the duty of every one of your band to use all his influence for Henry Clay."

Four years after Lucretia Mott was refused a seat at the World Anti-Slavery Convention in London and four years before the feminist announcement of the Seneca Falls Declaration of Principles, this teenager was writing to the men in her community:

> Although some think the ladies of this vicinity evince too much enthusiasm in the politics of the day, yet we cannot understand why we are to be debarred the privilege of participating in that which we feel to be of vital importance and which affects our happiness and welfare as much as yours; for certainly we as warmly wish the continuation of our country's glory, and that the lustre of its fame may not be dimmed, as any of your warmest partisans.

Unfortunately the community's reaction to this statement will never by known.

Within the month Slocum Howland decided to send Emily to a private school in Philadelphia. One of Slocum's reasons for this action may have been to remove Emily temporarily from community censure or ridicule which undoubtedly arose from her public expression of unorthodox feminist opinions.

Instead of enrolling Emily in a sheltered finishing school, Slocum placed her in the radically feminist environment of Mary Grew's school for young women. Mary Grew was a well-known and respected abolitionist with a soft-spoken gentle manner and a kindly face—favorable factors which may have influenced Slocum's decision. But Mary Grew's reputation also rested on her dedication to feminist principles. When Slocum enrolled Emily in Mary Grew's school, he may have been supporting his daughter in her feminist convictions in his quiet unobtrusive yet effective manner.

Emily, from the first, saw Mary Grew as a strong, independent woman who courageously bore witness to her belief in the equality of both females and blacks. Emily also perceived Grew's associate Margaret Jones Burleigh in this light. Margaret Burleigh was the sister-in-law of the eccentric abolitionist Charles Burleigh and was Mary Grew's closest friend. She taught the older students in Grew's school, including Emily. Together, Burleigh and Grew drew around them a closeknit group of friends and students committed to an active involvement in the dual reforms of abolition and women's rights. Radical abolitionists, Quaker lecturers and ministers, and fiery speakers visited the Grew home and soon Emily was meeting people such as Lucretia and James Mott, Sarah Pugh, and Sallie Holley. Her education became basic lessons in the various forms of urban social activism.

The abolitionists visiting Sherwood had initiated Emily into the world of the nineteenth century reformer; Grew and Burleigh took Emily one step further along the road. Emily had argued for women's political equality prior to her stay in Philadelphia, but in Burleigh and Grew she found mature activists who could provide her with the intellectual and emotional support needed to nurture and maintain an evolving mature feminist ideology. These months brought enthusiasms, happiness and freedom into Emily's life, but her euphoric state came to an abrupt end before her eighteenth birthday. Slocum ordered her home—the only time he actively inter-fered with the direction of Emily's interests and activities.

Why did Slocum abandon his policy of non-interference at this time? It doesn't seem likely that he would have become disturbed to find Emily receiving support for feminist beliefs since he himself subscribed to the Quaker testimony of human equality and knew of Grew's national feminist reputation. Emily did suggest a reason for her father's unusual behavior—a reason which shows the pervasive influence of society even upon Slocum Howland whose whole life seemed deeply immersed in the beliefs and practices of the Society of Friends.

> It was a heartbreak to give up school. But in those days it was not considered an advantage for a woman to have an education; so I came home and tried to live. Nobody can tell the unspeakable misery of a young person who has a vision before her and has to live below it.

Emily was bitterly disappointed and depressed over his action. Her father had exhibited blatant insensitivity to the needs and wants

*A subdued Emily after her return from feminist Mary
Grew's school in Philadelphia. (Courtesy Friends
Historical Library of Swarthmore College)*

of his young daughter. It was an insensitivity Emily would never
forget.

Emily busied herself by continuing her study of French and found
solace in looking for wild flowers, analyzing and pressing them for
her herbarium. She began to paint and sketch more frequently and
found that she was quite talented in protraiture as well in analytical
botanical reproductions. Slocum permitted her to accompany him to
the annual meetings in New York of the American Anti-Slavery
Society, there listening to the eloquence of Wendell Phillips and the
zealous orations of William Lloyd Garrison. At rare intervals a slave

traveling along the Underground Railroad would arrive at the Howland home to be secreted there until safe passage to the next station was guaranteed.

At the age of seventeen Emily found that she was living a paradox; although she was keenly alive to the historical events of this period, and their significance to her country, she was tied by the bonds of custom to a way of life that denied her active participation in those events. Emily began to feel that rather than promoting woman's equality in all spheres, the Society of Friends was confining her to the home, without proper education and within the strict and narrow lines of the sect. By circumscribing the range of her experience these limitations promoted heightened intensity of feeling yet afforded feeble outlets for such activities and sympathies. Emily began to feel that life was both purposeless and wasting for her. Contrary to the edicts of the Society and society, she began looking for but was unable to find "forbidden fields ripening for even (her) small sickle."

In these years Emily could not articulate her needs, dissatisfaction and discontent as succinctly as she did in maturity. On the evening before her eighteenth birthday Emily despondently turned, not to her mother Hannah or her dear friend and teacher Susanna Marriott, but to paper and pen which would be her closest friend and confidant for the next eighty-four years. Her first entries in her journal fail to reflect the full intensity with which she felt the limitations placed upon her as a young, rural, Quaker woman. At times her words were typical of the poetic musing found in other adolescent female journals. Yet she did place unusual emphasis on one important poetic phrase. In trying to depict the discontent and conflict she felt in her present way of life she wrote that her "brilliant fancies of imagination" were one means of coping with this internal conflict. She withdrew into her imagination.

Now she began to spend much time alone even when physically in the company of others. More than once the meetings for worship and business seemed wearisome to her and caused her frequent headaches; she began to withdraw further from her fellow Friends. The words of the *National Anti-Slavery Standard* and Garrison's *Liberator* held even more meaning to her than her Society's *Friend*. Admitting that the sect had many testimonies and principles that were excellent, Emily felt that they were offset by restrictions that were now galling and of little value to her. Although she continued to be outwardly obedient to the conventions of the community and the Friends, inwardly she was spinning fantasies of action which would be acted out, step by step, in the years to come.

In the final years of her teens, Emily confined herself to the lighter domestic chores in her parents' home, efficiently running the household when her mother was absent. She nursed ailing or dying friends and relatives, visiting among the family for varying lengths of time. Small signs of discontent and non-conformity to this domestic role appear; she laughingly began to attack the necessity of marriage for women in correspondence with her close friend and future sister-in-law Hannah Letchworth, but eventually called a truce to what became a serious argument on this subject. Her impatience with the restrictions of the Friends in worship, dress and custom and her flirtation with other than Quakerly ways is barely veiled in a letter to her mother in 1846. More noticeably, with each year her depression lengthened. "And yet another year has circled around my life's pathway—tonight I take leave of eighteen—a painful melancholy change does the past year bear in its expiring train, I could not then have thought that an impending cloud was so soon to darken my life's young dream."

The essence of this impending cloud very possibly was the "vain, bitter regrets for mispent lost time, yes, lost time, squandered what no price can recover, no useless repinings can recall one single moment of the squandered years!" The small intense child had grown to be a young woman and that marked intensity was even more noticeable in the young adult. Emily's yearly birthday essays were humorless, bitter, self-recriminatory epistles detailing the search of this young woman for a viable identity. The anguish can be felt over a century's time when reading Howland's cry: "What am I now? But little than I anticipated, and judging the future by the past what have I to hope but a similar series of regrets for I have not the energy, the moral force to reach the goal of my desired."

Emily portrayed herself as living a pained, dulled existence in late adolescence, all the while yearning for the energy necessary to relieve this condition. But one of her contemporaries did not share Emily's perception of herself or life in Sherwood. Justus Allen, a twenty-five year old neighbor, in fact, was impressed with Emily as well as with the lively pace of life in Sherwood during the late 1840s. Articulate, sensitive and intelligent, Justus was involved in the meetings of the Sons of Temperance at the Corners; he visited with the Letchworths and Howlands and threw himself into the activities of the Literary League where discussions of ethical and political questions was commonplace. Slavery, the perfectability of humans, the presidential elections, and the study of the law were just some of the topics touched in these evening conversations. And more than once Justus mentioned Emily Howland's name in his diary. A representative entry can be found under July 19, 1848:

> Called on Emily Howland this afternoon, a source to me of much profound satisfaction, I feel assured of something invaluable in the few moments I spend in her company.

Emily was a young woman capable of intellectual discussion and friendly conversation but perhaps more than that. Justus Allen saw additional dimensions to his neighbor and friend Emily. Later that summer, Justus, Emily and twenty-six young men and women traveled to the Cascades, a picnic ground on Owasco Lake. He describes Emily busy setting tables, furnishing food, riding on the lake, singing and listening to music in a relaxed and carefree manner with him. Through Justus's eyes, Emily is seen standing free from her relentless self-reproachment if only for brief moments.

In her journals Emily rarely touched upon her relationships with her friends or with her family. When Justus Allen died an untimely death in 1849 Emily mentioned only that one of her early associates had died. Still she may have been more moved than the entry shows. She asks why her life "so useless should ever have been granted or why perpetuated while others more valuable, more brilliant, have long since been gathered to an early grave."

In her twentieth year, Emily finally began to view the present less as a vacuum and more as a time for action. Attempting to shake off her despondency and become more concerned with the present, Emily entered the genteel world of rural philanthropy. She became involved collecting clothing from the community for fugitive slaves in Dawn Mills, Canada, and sewing for the county orphans with the Young Ladies Sewing Society. Although far from challenging, these activities gave her a needed sense of direction. She turned to her journal to confide that she had begun to find "a strong determination to do my duty, to fill up the measure of my existence and so far as possible to fill my allotted sphere if I can but find that uncertain place."

Her search for identity was far from over and she would step into many roles looking for "that allotted sphere" but this was the last time such total self-abnegation would appear. She recognized and was now ready to cope in a more positive manner with the painful discrepancy between reality and her fantasies. "I am more reconciled to myself and the world and I am learning charity—learning to search for excellence rather than faults."

Instead of turning with hostility inward upon herself as in the past, Emily was now trying to gather the strength needed to challenge the circumscribed role she felt was placed upon her by her family, her sect and her community.

2

The Passage

Winters in the Finger Lake region of New York are cold, harsh and filled with frequent snowstorms. During the winter of 1851 as the snow continued to drift across the open farm fields surrounding Sherwood Emily Howland made a decision to leave her parents' home. With their permission, Emily was embarking on a "search for excellence" which would lead her to Mary Robinson's school in Philadelphia.

As she took her leave from Hannah and Slocum, Emily's thoughts were turned fully on finding one way of making her empty life more purposeful. She did not need to teach for a living since her father provided for all her material needs. Knowing that Slocum objected to her pursuing a formal education, Emily felt that at last she had found a solution to this dilemma. By enrolling in Mary Robinson's school, she could devote herself to the life and luxury of being an informal scholar by taking tutored courses and listening to lectures which would enrich her life.

This approach met with Slocum's tacit approval but Emily soon became aware of strong maternal disapproval. Hannah Howland repeatedly reminded Emily of her daughter's "advanced age" although she did admit that no one was too old to learn. Hannah also made veiled references to the formidable sacrifice she was undergoing during her daughter's thoughtless absence. Even with the apparent conflict, Emily managed to pack her baggage and journey to Philadelphia not only during this winter but also for the next six winters. Every year for the three winter months, she would make the difficult eighteen hour trip from Sherwood to Philadelphia by lake boat and crowded uncomfortable trains. Once settled into her comfortably furnished boarding house in the center of the city, Emily would fill her winter daylight hours with Latin, German and botany classes while occupying her evenings with lectures at the Female Medical College, the local antislavery society and the Ethical Union.

Emily felt that her experience with this unstructured educational process would help to alleviate her sense of dissatisfaction and discontent with her relatively directionless position as an adult daughter living with her parents. She had carefully examined the one role open to her within her community—a religious minister within the Society of Friends—and frankly admitted that she did not feel "called" to such a vocation. She wholeheartedly endorsed the Quaker belief in the "unmistakeable birthright of women to do anything which God gave them power to do in any field to which they were called by the voice in their own souls." But unlike two of her fellow Quakers, Lucretia Mott and Abby Kelley Foster, Emily questioned her spiritual leading and knew that she had not been chosen to toil with them in this field. She saw the religious ministry as prestigious, fulfilling and liberating since women, both married and single, were able to obtain a degree of freedom, mobility and equality unknown and generally unacceptable for women outside the Society of Friends.

But in turning away from this calling within the Society, Emily actually did not wander far from the Quaker fold; she repeatedly returned to those Quaker friends in Philadelphia whose activism and ideas had touched her so deeply during her formative teenage years. Along with her friends in the circle surrounding Mary Grew and Margaret Burleigh, Emily hoped that she could begin to combine educational and reformist concerns and tackle intellectual and moral challenges after her long struggle to find "this pathway to maturity."

Her companions in Philadelphia during the next six winters were primarily women whose acquaintance Emily had first made at Mary Grew's a decade before. The influence that Mary Grew, Margaret Jones Burleigh, Mary Reed, Mary Robinson, Sallie Holley, Caroline F. Putnam, Gulie Jones, Ellen Child and Cornelia Hancock had upon her cannot be understated. These women formed the core of a female friendship network that was also an intellectual community and an activist group. Emily thought of these nine women and herself as the creators of an emerging, radical female ideology based upon their intellectual concern with two untenable conditions within American society—the inferior positions of both women and blacks. The majority of these women were pragmatists dissatisfied with attempting only to formulate tenets for an ideal society. Wishing to effect change, many of them began to write and lecture upon the twin evils in their midst. Acting in accord with their new-found radicalism, they purposefully deviated from the quiet, passive, more traditional roles held by the majority of women within nineteenth century America. Functioning in a unique position for females—as intellectual reformers—they also called themselves members of a loving network of friends.

Emily was both frightened and exhilirated by this shared vision of sisterhood. Through education, writing and speaking, women, including herself, could begin to change their roles, their relationships and their daily lives. Reformers outside this group soon grasped Emily's vision and began to share her understanding of the threefold bonds of love, reform and scholarship existing between and among these women. One of them saw this collection of unusual women as, "large-brained . . . politically astute . . . wise . . . devoted to one another with that affection *passing the love of men.*"

Emily looked fondly toward her former teachers, Mary Grew and Margaret Burleigh, for intellectual, moral and spiritual guidance. These two inseparable friends were in their second decade of working against slavery and for women's rights within the United States. While Mary Grew traveled on the lecture circuit making speeches at local Northern antislavery societies, Margaret Burleigh successfully ran her school attempting to instill in her young students a concern for the injustices of slavery and female inequality. Yet this was just one aspect of their tremendously active life for both Grew and Burleigh considered themselves to be scholars as well as teachers. An informal education process was their only outlet since higher formal education was virtually closed to these women at midcentury. They joined with other women who sought intellectual stimulation. With an ingenuity born of necessity they attended and later sponsored public lecture series, patronized private formerly male associations such as the Ethical Union and the Philadelphia

Men's Moral Society and informally attended local college courses officially closed to females.

They directed Emily's studies, provided tutors in languages, arranged trips to museums, reform societies, college classes and public lectures with such rapidity and enthusiasm that Emily, at first, had trouble adjusting to this new and exciting environment. In letters during 1851 to her old friend and new sister-in-law, Hannah Letchworth Howland, Emily commented frequently on the sudden change that had taken place in her life after leaving the comparative isolation of tiny rural Sherwood for the challenging, stimulating life in crowded cosmopolitan Philadelphia. Emily felt comfortable with Burleigh and Grew as guides in this new world filled with strange sights, sounds and concerns, but this did not mean that other women were unable to occupy important positions in Emily's new life. Her new tutor, Mary Robinson, soon became a close and respected friend. Mary was devoted to teaching and the intellectual development of the young women in her care. More concerned with women's rights than with abolition, Mary hoped to change the small portion of society in which she came in daily contact by raising a feminist consciousness in her students through her teaching.

Another teaching friend was Mary Reed, a young woman who worked with Mary Robinson and had been part of the Grew circle since the early 1840s. Mary and Emily began to spend many hours comfortably in one another's company. Mary had strayed from the Society of Friends and had been flirting with Unitarian ideas. Emily who had attended Unitarian services while visiting relatives a few years earlier now began to visit the local Unitarian churches with Mary Reed, exploring more deeply her creeds and beliefs. This brief excursion outside of Quakerism ended with Emily's admission that she was drawn more by the special visiting speakers such as Dr. Longfellow, Henry Ward Beecher, William E. Channing and Wendell Phillips than by a burgeoning theological compatibility with Unitarianism.

Mary Reed and Mary Robinson were perhaps the most religious and least politically oriented members of the group. They felt that teaching was the highest calling a woman could attain for religious as well as intellectual reasons. They wanted to spend their lives attempting to improve their minds as well as the minds of those around them in obedience to God's will. Neither were radical active reformers in the mold of Grew and Burleigh. Reed and Robinson held only nominal membership in the local reform societies for temperance and abolition, but they were concerned with bringing about changes in the popular image of women. In a radical departure from the stereotype of the prim maiden schoolmistress, they enthusiastically adopted the Bloomer dress. Rather than wear it only in the confines of their homes as many feminist did, Reed and Robinson even wore the dress while teaching. It is uncertain if Emily also occasionally adopted this comfortable, loose-fitting yet controversial costume. Reed and Robinson with their unusual intellectual outlook, dressed in their Bloomer outfits, effectively conveyed an image of the single woman as an independent, capable and contributing, if controversial, member of society.

Emily gained a great deal from her association with both Reed and Robinson while assisting them in their capacity as helpmates to those active, organization women in the abolition, women's rights, temperance and "moral purity" movements. Mary Robinson's Germantown home for years was a haven for local and national speakers on the reform lecture circuit. Mary Reed, never economically secure enough to own a home of her own, organized yearly winter rentals at her Philadelphia boarding house to accommodate the female reformers traveling from city to city on organization business. There Emily participated with these women in long satisfying discussions on literature, art, music, scientific discoveries, and philosophy.

Sallie Holley and Caroline F. Putnam were two organization women who needed such intellectual respite from the intense political atmosphere in which they thrived. Since the 1840s Holley and Putnam had been virtually inseparable as they worked with the radical abolitionists and for women's rights. Holley and Putnam, like Howland, hailed from central New York and were the only members not permanent residents of Philadelphia. Emily was immediately drawn to Carrie Putnam, the less publicly-known of this dynamic couple, for in Carrie Emily felt that she had found a similarly intense young woman "searching and finding her allotted sphere."

Carrie Putnam had "abandoned her soul to the great cause of freedom for the slave" and in doing so had met the emotional, hard-driving and flamboyant Sallie Holley. An eloquent speaker, Sallie Holley spent almost twenty years of her life lecturing on the evils of slavery while Carrie Putnam quietly arranged practical, day-to-day details of their life on the lecturing and convention circuit. Although very close to radical abolitionists and feminists, such as Gerritt Smith, Sallie Holley and Carrie Putnam considered themselves tied by equally strong bonds to the Philadelphia Grew group. Perhaps that unique intellectual atmosphere and supportive warmth pervading the Grew group which drew Emily each winter to Philadelphia similarly attracted these two social activists.

Emily admired Holley and Putnam's ability to be thinkers, planners and idealists as they battled against the inequality of women and blacks. They openly shared and reinforced a common, radical, intellectual female ideology based on a determined concern to bring about social change which helped Emily to see reform as a double-edged sword with women's rights on one side and abolitionism on the other. With these two women's help, Emily soon shared their conviction that this sword was to be held in women's hands and that the reform words were to come from women's hearts and mouths as together they reached toward a higher plane of thought and action with God behind them. Unlike Emily, Sallie and Carrie felt "called by a Divine voice" to plead the slaves' and the women's cause publicly. Sallie had been trained to become an effective, emotional lecturer. The eloquent speaker, Abby Kelley Foster, on hearing Holley speak wrote that she laid "prostrate before the throne of God, weeping with thankfulness and joy that (now), when I am worn out, He has raised up one who pleads (for us) as you have done so powerfully tonight."

Three other women deserve mention as valuable if relatively unknown members of Emily's Philadelphia friends. Gulie Jones, Margaret Burleigh's sister, was a Friend sympathetic to the abolition, temperance and women's rights movements. Her name appears frequently in Emily's journal and letters as a participant in the informal meetings and visits which took place among the resident Philadelphia group.

Ellen Child, the only one of the group during this period who was married (with a young, active family) managed to become involved in antislavery work through her friendship with fellow Friend, Lucretia Mott. Emily Howland spent many hours in the Child's home discussing the ethical and moral issues involved in slavery and women's rights. Child, Howland and Reed also happened to share an enthusiasm for botany and on more than one occasion they went off to the swamplands of New Jersey to find rare specimens for their prized herbariums.

Ellen Child's sister, Cornelia Hancock, needs no introduction for she numbers among the few well-known Civil War nurses. During the 1850s she was a marginal member of this network, joining the groups activities only during the sporadic visits to her sister Ellen's home. In fact, Emily did not meet Cornelia until the second year of the Civil War when Emily helped place her at the Contraband Camp Hospital in Washington, D.C.. They were to become great friends.

Excepting Ellen Child, the most peripheral member of the group over time, they were eight single women who had consciously chosen to remain unmarried—sometimes in the face of family disapproval and in many cases community rejection, hostility or ridicule. Emily Howland often commented on the emotional support and encouragement they provided one another as budding or full-blossomed radical female intellectual-reformers. With this group Emily shared life-long loving relationships which ended only with death. Although these women were to be geographically separated for long periods of time in later life, their love and concern for one another continued unabated over four decades. When a member became seriously ill, others within the group traveled to nurse her. They rested from their work together at New York water-cures and southern New Jersey sanitariums, traveled abroad in small groups and pairs to enrich their intellectual life, and could be counted on to rush to the side of any member experiencing vocational or personal problems. The more affluent members helped to support their less fortunate sisters. When death occurred, they mourned together and wrote loving testimonies and memorials in honor of the departed member of their group. This shared concern was pervasive entering into all facets of the members lives—financial, spiritual, intellectual and emotional. In their roles as older single women, they no longer could look to their nuclear family of origin for assistance in these essentially familial responsibilities. Instead, the members of this group over time began to assume the traditional economic, social and moral responsibilities and functions of the nuclear family.

When Margaret Jones Burleigh wrote, "Don't forget me, dear Emily, for thou art one of the stars in my sky," she could have been writing this to any of the other nine women for each held a distinct place in the other's esteem. Emily found that these women were opening new horizons to her and to one another in the areas of social concerns and intellectual development. She realized also that they more than any others were responsible for changing her perspective of herself. She no longer viewed herself solely as comforter to her parents in their declining years but saw herself as a link in an intellectual community of worldly women.

In Sherwood, Emily's sister-in-law Hannah recognized this awakening in her and encouraged her to persevere, lightening Emily's role at home by caring for her ailing mother. Emily must have felt herself in the midst of a metamorphis during these years: her identity among her friends in Sherwood was also undergoing a change. With just a touch of awe, one young friend wrote to Emily: "You are now strongly given to dwell on the invisible and hidden things of our existence; you are disposed to scan it to its remotest foundation and compare it with our present being and with this comes the conflict and change."

Emily was happiest when she could briefly rejoin the circle in Philadelphia each winter; the long months spent at home doing household tasks and charity work were times of introspection. She corresponded regularly with the Philadelphia network. Her remarks in her journals make it clear that these letters barely sustained her through the long months. She felt a need to delve into a variety of subjects in great detail, causing one Philadelphian to exclaim: "I have been trying to *answer* thy letter but I cannot grasp all the themes though I have tried to touch the most prominent. Thy letters give me a good deal of inward exhaustion."

In addition to giving a good deal of inward exhaustion, Emily also demanded an equal amount of inward strength in her friends as well as herself. She began to speak openly of her alignment with the more radical abolitionists taking the unpopular stance of supporting them as "Fearless and strong with enthusiasm and eloquence without parallel in any land on the earth." She was not afraid to state that the nation was being threatened by an arrogant and wicked slave-power and that slavery was a type of authority forbidden by God and the slaveholder both evil and intolerable for placing himself in the sinful position of contending against divine sovereignty. Emily was now feeling her way less cautiously into "entering this Holy War against American Slavery."

Concurrently, into every possible communication she inserted her belief in women's right to equal freedom with men particularly in the economic and political spheres. The Holy War against American Slavery came first at this time, the "tyranny of the 'Lords of Creation'" ran a very close second.

Emily's openness apparently did not threaten the men and women of Sherwood for they began to seek her advice on items as far-ranging as the wording of presidential and congressional petitions to political strategy discussions by the local abolitionist groups. This new role became another factor in the delicate balance of her allegiance between her rural birthplace and her loving network in the city. She had not yet come to a commitment to devoting her life to working for social change. Despite the fervor of her rhetoric, she had taken only small steps in the direction of active radicalism. Fear and self-doubting were still present.

> Why I used to think that at twenty-five every idle day dream, every air castle would be expurgated from my foolish head, but I am as much their victim as ever; they assume a little different form as my tastes and views change but they are the same insidious baneful things that ever they were. Indeed they are the foes which I now must fight they are my worst ones and if they hold their sway well preclude all hopes of soul progress.

Emily used the term "soul progress" to describe her search for wisdom and knowledge as the rewards of labor and thought. She felt that when the mind rose to higher things, to nobleness or goodness, through the eradication of evil towards blacks and women, only then had one made real progress in the journey to the final home after death. Unlike many of her friends in Philadelphia, Emily felt that she had been unsuccessful in this search to integrate her personal and political visions and philosophies.

Sallie Holley was an agent for the Massachusetts Anti-Slavery Society, lecturing in the Northeast and West at a frantic pace while filling columns of the *Liberator* and *Anti-Slavery Standard* with reams of her writings. Carrie Putnam, Holley's ever faithful friend, accompanied her organizing the myriad details encountered on the lecture circuit. Mary Grew was continuing the seminal abolitionist work she had been accomplishing for almost two decades with the support and encouragement of Margaret Burleigh. Mary Robinson, and to a lesser extent Mary Reed, were occupied in imparting to their female classes feminist principles which governed their own thoughts and actions. Holding friendships with women such as these it is not surprising to find Emily writing at the close of 1856:

> I believe I am ripe for a new chapter of human experience more comprehensive and varied than any gone before and I think it is at hand. I have the fullest faith in this, I see and feel it and know it will come perhaps within the bounds of the present year for thus far what was needful for me has been provided. We shall see.

Although Emily had no more than a vague intuition regarding the events that were to unfold for her in the next year the sense of waste and regret voiced so often in the past were gone.

At the close of winter Myrtilla Miner visited the home of Margaret Burleigh. Miner who was born in the "burned-over district" of New York had taught in the home of a slaveholder in Mississippi when a young woman. The institution of slavery roused within her such antipathy that she returned north with a determination to teach black children. Deciding on Washington, D.C. as the place for her trial and ignoring the negative reactions to this reckless and rather visionary scheme she established a school for economically stable black females. With the aid of abolitionist members of Congress, wealthy Philadelphia Friends as trustees and a modest tuition charge her school on the outskirts of the capital was a showplace for a certain antislavery faction of that city.

When Miner's health deteriorated in the mid-1850s, requiring extensive visits to the Elmira Water Cure, the school was conducted by upper-middle class teachers who could afford to volunteer their services to this cause. Miner spent increasingly large portions of time away from Washington in search of better health and soliciting aid for her economically weak enterprise. It was on one of these latter trips to Philadelphia that Emily first heard of Myrtilla Miner and the work she had in progress. She was not present when Miner visited Margaret Burleigh but Margaret gave her a full description of their talk including the information that Miner was in quest of a teacher for her school. Emily later wrote: "The idea of offering myself struck me and I exclaimed 'I should like to go.' I was leading the aimless life that was required of young women, the more imperative necessity of being employed to ensure health of body and mind was neither recognized nor understood." But twenty months passed before this impulsive statement came to fruition. Meanwhile a fascinating series of letters circulated among Emily's friends and relatives. The topic most frequently discussed was the feasibility of Emily leaving home to teach in a school for blacks in the slaveholding capital. From over a century's distance it is difficult to gain the perspective of the intricacies of this decision. That this was a momentous step for an ardent abolitionist and feminist to take may seem implausible to the twentieth century mind. Yet, in 1856 Emily's friends, other than those in the Philadelphia network and Emily herself, viewed teaching children of another race in Washington as bizarre behavior even for a woman of her background and persuasion. They found it unthinkable for a young woman living a largely sheltered life in an upper-middle class family in rural New York to travel alone on an uncomfortable three-day journey by boat and train to Washington. There she would be the sole white inhabitant of a simple wooden schoolhouse sitting on the outskirts of Georgetown. Furthermore, this school had been and continued to be a center of controversy within the immediate community as well as within Washington political circles. Mobs, threats, open contempt and hostility and financial difficulties were daily worries of the white teachers who had dared to teach female children of another race.

Emily's idea was not even taken seriously by her New York friends and neighbors; first she was gently humored, while Margaret Burleigh as spokeswoman for the Grew network told her that "the plan seems altogether rational and feasible for in such a position thee would impart and receive, and thy soul demands both of these."

Emily's brothers, William and Benjamin, had originally followed Slocum's policy of a "wholesome letting alone" with their sister. They showed her in small ways their concern but for the most part remained distant yet caring. Then after younger brother Benjamin wrote a surprisingly warm and supportive letter to Emily actively encouraging her to take this step, Emily took courage from his words and began to lay more definite plans. Benjamin had apparently touched upon an important dynamic in Emily's struggle to realize her potential. A warm, comfortable relationship between them soon

developed so that Benjamin felt free to express such thoughts as
these to his sister:

> Well I am sincerely glad that thee had finally decided to do
> what thee ought (for thy own happiness) to have done long ago.
> As for what the world may say, I wouldn't care a straw and I
> rather think thee doesn't, so I will give no arguments to prove
> why this should be so—the world is a vain, meddlesome fool,
> whose opinions are not worth minding in such a case as this,
> where there is nothing but a matter of propriety in question.

Ednah Thomas, a close friend and neighbor, was soon working to
set up a meeting between Howland and Miner during the fall of 1856
while Miner was visiting in the area. Margaret Burleigh and Mary
Grew wrote to Miner throughout the fall discussing compensation
and living arrangements in Washington on their friend Emily's
behalf. It was not until October 28, 1856 that Emily finally
addressed herself directly to Myrtilla Miner, offering to become an
assistant in her school and acknowledging Burleigh's invaluable
assistance in this matter. Emily, with refreshing honesty, readily
admitted that while she had the approval of certain friends, she
feared the censure of others.

> I take the liberty of writing you now myself, to make a request
> which may seem very strange to you, and may lead you to think
> me foolishly fastidious, which may be true. The request is this,
> that you will not mention my proposition in Union Springs, the
> reason this, I have many acquaintances there, some of them
> your friends also, and it would be excessively annoying to me to
> have this project of mine become the subject of remark among
> them, and from them spread wherever I am known and greet
> me at every stop; as any thing out of the usual track never fails
> to excite the ridicule of some at one's folly, the censure of others
> and the wonder of all. As I have a great dread of being talked
> about I think I could hardly endure such an ordeal, when I am
> fairly embarked, if ever, of course it will be known but then I
> shall be beyond the reach of talk and shall not heed them.

Admitting to Miner that she was a novice in teaching, equipped
only with an earnest desire and determination to work and be useful,
Emily next began what she termed her preparation for her chosen

vocation. During the winter of 1856–57, she began to spend increasing amounts of time in Auburn, the nearest large town, telling her mother that she was visiting with friends. In actuality she was taking lessons while seeking an apprenticeship as a teacher. Emily felt that to arrive at her stated goal she had to overcome a twofold problem: to be capable and to be free to act. That winter was spent in making herself both. To become a teacher qualified to direct Miner's school was a far easier order than the second. After practice teaching for a month Howland felt that "although I cannot teach at all to my satisfaction, perhaps never shall, my trial thus far has brought a content I have not known for many long weary years. I long to be in my place for there it is with the poorest, most despised on earth. The longer I live the better I know this, the more I know that nothing short of such a verity can ever make life endurable to me."

But shadowing this contentment was a fear that her mother would not understand her need and would forbid her to pursue the course she had set for herself. Emily felt certain that her father by this time had obtained some knowledge of her plans and assumed that he would be more sympathetic to her plea than her mother. Throughout the spring and early summer Emily made feeble attempts but could not bring herself to discussing her plans and preparations with her mother. Finally in late June, in a letter to Margaret Burleigh, Emily compared herself to the prophets of old; she must walk through fire before her way would be clear. And the first test would be seeking Hannah Howland's permission.

As Emily now tried to prepare herself to act, Myrtilla Miner wrote:

> I think I told you I believed you *inspired* and, therefore, it is safe for you to act your own thoughts regardless of any human aid—for God will take care of you and deliver you. He will shut the lions' mouths that they cannot harm you. If you are the true Melanchthon of the cause, as I fully believe, your way will be made clear to you tho it seem dark to all other eyes.

Appropriately enough, while Wendell Phillips was delivering a stirring speech calling for Northern men and women to act with courage in the face of slavery, Emily Howland after a month's deliberation took the final step in her torturous decision. She wrote that extraordinary message of July 29, 1857 to her mother, acting in the

manner Phillips so eloquently advocated. By August 10th her
mother's reaction was recorded by Emily.

> Now comes the word 'I go'. My mother does not think of trying
> to prevent me tho' she thinks it's dreadful to have me go and
> leave them. A great many things tie me, claim my labor and
> thought here—for I have always been one of the little Dorrit's
> in a measure.

Myrtilla Miner like many of the women in Emily's Philadelphia
network believed that the female intellectual-activist should assume
masculine qualities exhibited by Melanchthon and the male Biblical
prophets. Emily speaking of her weakness in coming to terms with
her entry into active radicalism equated it with being female, a little
Dorrit, the pathetic waif in Charles Dickens' 1857 novel. Conversely
as she gained strength she saw herself as a modern-day Melanchthon, and in doing so was able to truly join her fellow reformers and
fully share in their social vision.

Emily rarely exhibited marked enthusiasm or exhiliration but as
she prepared to leave for Washington that summer, her spirits could
not be checked. Her radical female friends similarly rejoiced, sending her toward the Miner School with the belief that she would find
"peace and joyful freedom that comes to everyone who bears the
cross of duty laid by conscience on the soul." At last, Emily's "pent
up genius" would be able "to diffuse such genial gifts upon the
needy minds of 'Africa's sable daughters'." In this benevolent frame
of mind in September, 1857, Emily began to walk cautiously out of
the comfortable, closed world in Sherwood and into that unknown
world of Washington, D.C.

3

A Barque on the Ocean of Life

On the corner of 20th and N Streets in Washington stood a small white frame house facing the commons across a narrow dirt road. Inside the main room of the house thirty-eight young women between the ages of ten and twenty were seated at long tables listening quietly to the somewhat older woman who addressed them. Short in stature and of average weight, the speaker had an alert, kindly face. Although dressed plainly in somber gray with her thick brown hair swept behind her ears and into a loose knot at the base of her neck, the total effect was still one that belied this woman's thirty years. In sharp juxtaposition to an overall impression of gentleness were the woman's dark arching eyebrows and piercing eyes that seemed not to miss even the smallest detail in the room.

If Emily Howland felt any misgivings as she stood before her class this first day of school in October, 1857, it was unknown to her pupils as they listened to her words. She frankly told them why she offered herself as their teacher and of her ignorance of what she had undertaken to do. Not realizing that these pupils generally tested the power of a teacher before yielding obedience, she continued on, asking them to cooperate with her in the work that could be mutually useful and beneficial. Something in the straight-forwardness and simplicity of this appeal struck a responsive chord in these students and they seemingly decided to give this new teacher an opportunity to prove her sincerity without the usual trial. Perhaps the pupils' reaction to Emily was based on more than her earnestness. Emily much to her surprise saw seated before her not poor bondswomen, but adolescents who knew little of slavery in their own lives, from financially secure homes, many with skin as fair as their teacher. Urbane, sophisticated in the ways of the city and world to an extent far beyond that of their teacher, they quite possibly recognized the innocence and the limited knowledge of human nature this quiet women from the country evinced. Possibly, with children's intuition, they may have sensed how deeply their teacher felt about her own presence there. Perhaps they also sensed that this was a crucial moment in this woman's life; there is no doubt that Howland saw it so.

Emily's approach managed to arouse such interest in the black community that by the end of the first term the house was filled with students and the kitchen had to be pressed into service as an additional schoolroom. As an assistant in the school wrote proudly to Myrtilla Miner, "So many have applied for admittance to the school that Emily Howland was obliged to tell them to bring their own chairs, all the school chairs being occupied." Others spoke of the new spirit that had invaded the school after Emily's arrival. Unaware that the enthusiasm she was generating was unusual, Emily assumed that the students had always responded with this hearty interest. When she began to teach in October, Emily consciously modelled herself after Susanna Marriott, using the same methods and attitudes toward education that her teacher had so successfully instilled in her in her youth.

Emily's simple espousal in words, but more importantly in actions, of the equality of all persons were a welcome surprise to these young women who were familiar with the paternalism and latent racism of Myrtilla Miner and their two former teachers. Myrtilla Miner's contempt for the "degraded class" she was attempting to upraise was less veiled in her correspondence the longer her contact with them. The closer these free blacks came to attaining middle class status, the more threatened Miner felt, and the more hostile her behavior became. Rather than feeling rewarded when her students successfully attempted to reach the goals set forth, Miner lashed out with a sense of superiority, exposing a racism that might have surprised even her Southern slaveholding contemporaries.

Before Howland's arrival, when one of her students broke a

minor health rule of the school, Miner wrote to the parents "May your eyes be opened to comprehend what dreadful endurance is involved in the mission to raise a people who constantly turn back to their idols and sigh for the 'flesh pots of Egypt'." These parents, despite this insult, continued to send their two daughters to the school. Rather than taking this and similar comments at face value the black community may well have ignored them realizing that Miner was providing a unique service in education for black females in that city. Thus, the community that took advantage of the services offered by the school had to learn to recognize and handle the underlying attitudes of hostility and contempt if they wished their daughters to be educated.

No doubt Emily was surprised to find on her arrival in Washington not a degraded class of another race but "white children compelled to go to a colored school because the African taint in the blood could never be ignored." She perceived her students to be the children of Noah in sharp contrast with Miner's perception of them as the woolly children of Ham. Emily interjected the Quakerly principle of equality into her relationship with her pupils.

The first term Howland and Miner shared the upstairs chambers of the house, calling it the teachers' quarters. The two women viewed each other with mutual satisfaction and respect, giving no hint of the bitter feelings that were to erupt between them in later months. In fact, through Miner, a detailed description of those first few months is supplied.

> Do you wonder as do many others how we two women live here alone so far from town and friends with no protector but the Father? It is a real curiosity to many and I was amused with Dr. Dewey's wondering skeptical look when I asked him to come to dinner—when enjoying our cozy nice wholesome dinners, our friends seem to think this little hut a sort of magical 'Alladin's lamp'. Everything is so pioneer—like that upon looking about you see no place for anything especially when the 30 pupils which we daily have are closely stowed in. Miss Howland is a host in herself acting as housekeeper, teacher, scribe and prophet. I serving simply as prompter general of all extra niceties, yankee skill and economies discovered only by faith until proved in real life.

Miner insisted that there be two white persons present in the same room at all times, basing the reason for this order on the existing law in Washington which excluded the testimony of black witnesses in courts of justice. Miner lived in fear of "an uprising of the mob spirit directed against the school." This fear reflected the reality that had faced Prudence Crandall in her experimental school for black females in Connecticut two decades earlier, and which characterized the Washington white community in the 1850s; it also played a major part in the pattern of Miner's rampant paranoia.

The first open disagreement between the two women occurred when Miner requested Emily to keep a white teacher associated with her. Emily had been working with Emma Brown, a young black woman, as her assistant and was loathe to change this arrangement. Emma remained as assistant despite Miner's insistence that they were adding an element of danger to the operation of the school. There were daily incidents that served to reinforce Miner's fears and to draw Emily and Emma closer together. According to Emily a group of young white men began to rove about "daily over the commons with dogs and guns ready for any mischief. They often harassed the girls on their way to school or to their homes, jostling them off the sidewalk into the mud. or snatching their books."

On one occasion, just before the hour of closing school, approximately twenty appeared in force, lining up outside the yard in front of the house. Emily delayed dismissing her pupils until she saw that the men would bide their time. She admonished the girls to go quietly and deliberately out of the gate and past them without showing a sign of fear. She then went out and held the group's attention by talking with them until the students were well over the commons and could not be overtaken. Harassment virtually ended after this incident. Emily's commonsensical approach to these everyday occurrences provided a needed relief from the steady diet of fear of persecution with which Miner supplied the school.

When winter arrived Miner decided to travel, searching for both funds and better health. Emily, with Emma's help, continued to lead the school but in a direction subtly different from that of Miner's. She entered into her first close relationship with a black woman—one that was to become increasingly free from racial and class inequality inherent in such relationships at that time. Emma Brown moved into the teachers' quarters with Emily sharing the housekeeping and teaching responsibilities, as Emily had similarly helped Miner in the first school term. Together, they attended sessions of Congress, visited the Smithsonian and listened to sermons at the Unitarian church. Emma's opinion of Emily was unequivocal in its enthusiasm and admiration. "She is so good and kind, in fact I think her *everything* a human being *could* be."

Emma was not alone in regarding Emily in a highly positive light. To the surprise of students and assistant alike Emily, with the aid of Mr. Thomas the janitor, painted the house inside and out, after purchasing and mixing the paint herself. This seemingly unfeminine behavior drew the wrath of Myrtilla Miner but the applause of the expanded community of sixty scholars. "When you are away down the common, you can see the little cottage gleaming out like a city that is set on a hill," Emma Brown wrote Myrtilla Miner. But troubles were to come to the city on the hill very shortly.

In June, Emily received an urgent plea from her mother to come home and "pour the balm of consolation in the hearts of thy stripped family." Two deaths had recently occurred within the family and Hannah saw this as an excellent opportunity to bring Emily home from an occupation she neither understood nor approved. What Hannah did not know was that Emily needed to leave Washington at that time. As Emma Brown noted, "Not being accustomed to teaching, it soon wore her down. Though I miss her sadly I am glad for her sake that she has gone. For some weeks before her departure she lost her appetite and grew rather nervous."

Emily's family had moved into a larger home that spring, located on the Ridge Road south of the Corners. Emily had been looking forward to seeing her family settled in this house and was anxious to visit with her friends who had corresponded so faithfully with her over the past year. She admitted to her exhaustion and yet was confused by her weakness. "O I am of no more value in a quiet life than a bell never suffered to ring. I fancy I feel very much as such an instrument of sound must. When not on duty—a great dangling thing of no sort of use."

Yet she remained off duty at home for five months, caring for her mother who continued to be in poor health, even while writing that she was determined to return to Washington. The old conflict centering around her freedom to act arose again. Once home in Sherwood, Emily stopped receiving the admiration and respect granted her by her Washington and Philadelphia circles. Her old neighbors took a far different and less understanding view of her reformist career. As one matron remarked with bemusement, "It is remarkable that she should have felt so strongly impelled to leave all the enjoyments of her home, an only daughter, and thro strong opposition from her friends, go on such a mission." Even her dear Auburn friend Phebe Coffin implored her not to labor for such a cause and considered the situation Emily placed herself in as unendurable. Rare was the friend in Cayuga County who understood and encouraged her as Carrie Putnam did.

> I shall be most of all eager to hear your own joys, hopes, successes, and trials, the *triumph* as the old hymn says, of the prophets, I know you too 'see' from afar. Your joint school and house-keeping (in Washington) is *far more* than the ordinary mode of domesticity—the family proper.

One childhood friend did agree with Putnam however, even believing that the teaching experience in Washington was valuable enough to join Emily in her work. In October 1858 Emily Howland and that friend, Anna Searing, left Sherwood together to return to Washington and Myrtilla Miner's school. They persuaded Emma Brown to stay on as an advanced student as well as assistant and worked to build the number of attending students. Their efforts met with the satisfaction of at least one of the trustees, Samuel J. Bowen.

> Miss Howland is teaching again and I understand she is more than ever convinced of the success of the undertaking. I shall see her soon and learn what her resolutions are as to remaining longer than next spring.

If Myrtilla Miner was pleased with this information, her correspondence did not reflect it. Her behavior toward Emily, Anna and Emma became erratic, calling for them to leave their positions at the end of the term on one day and berating them for not assuming more long term responsibilities the next. In addition Miner had begun to draw elaborate plans for a costly new school building. This was occurring at a time when the wealthy fund raisers and benefactors of the school were questioning her bizarre spiritualist experiments with clairvoyants and magnetic healers. Concurrently Miner's capability for making sound decisions was under investigation by the school's trustees, the result of which was a bitter fight between Miner and the board culminating in the resignation of three key trustees.

As Miner's behavior became more suspect, the trustees and Washington friends of the school began to confide in Howland, expressing their doubts and attendant difficulties with Miner. Within a short time Emily became a trusted member of a small social circle composed of the Breeds, Danas, Bowens and, at times, the Sewards. William H. Seward was the United States Senator from New York. His wife, Fanny Seward, first met Emily when they were schoolmates in Aurora and their friendship continued despite geographic separations. The Breeds were friends of Ellen Child's physician husband, but little is known about the Breeds or the Danas before the Civil War. They appear to have been part of the government community in Georgetown, active abolitionists and interested in black education in the city. Although not trustees of the Miner school, they nevertheless willingly became enmeshed in the internal affairs of the school. The Bowens, however, were Emily's closest friends in the Washington white community. Samuel Bowen was a Miner school trustee, a fellow Friend and abolitionist, and a warm perceptive person who implicitly understood the problems Emily faced daily. The Bowen home was open to Emily and during these years she dined and was entertained there frequently.

It was into this community of supportive friends that Miner unexpectedly reappeared in early March. Behaving somewhat peculiarly Miner clearly saw Emily as a personal threat and announced her plans to regain control of the school. A confused Emily did not understand this newest turn in Miner's behavior and found herself unable to cope with being the prime suspect in Miner's paranoia. It is not surprising that shortly after Miner's announcement the two women parted, both disillusioned and angry. Without funds, equipment and teachers, Miner was forced to close the school in 1860. With the approach of war and continuing illness, Miner went to California, supporting herself as a spiritualist and healer. Within five years she died of tuberculosis and was buried in Washington, D.C.

Her loyalty continuing to fluctuate between reformist friends and family, Emily elected at this point not to return to Philadelphia nor to remain with sympathetic friends in the District of Columbia, but to go back to Sherwood. Although she vowed not to return to her former way of life, Emily's return to Sherwood effectively marks the beginning of a three year hiatus from reformist activities. It heralds as well a period of prolonged sex-role conflict for her. When Emily chose the socially unacceptable female role alternative of teaching young black women in Washington, she had cast her lot with the radical feminists and abolitionists and it was assumed that she wholeheartedly believed in the equally radical ideologies underlying her new non-traditional position within nineteenth century American society. Her introduction to reformist activities at Myrtilla Miner's school, however, proceeded to shatter some of her preconceived beliefs regarding blacks, education and, most important, certain of her fellow female reformers.

Her experience in Washington and her relationship with Myrtilla Miner particularly may well have helped to govern her subsequent behavior in Sherwood over the next three years. When she journeyed to Washington, she felt she had finally begun to express her needs for autonomy, independence and dominance. More significantly she apparently felt that she had resolved the conflict of wholeheartedly endorsing a socially deviant role for herself. Upon her arrival in Washington, she sought satisfying and fulfilling relationships based on shared abolitionist and feminists interests. Rather than finding a sisterhood with her mentor Myrtilla Miner, however, the contact proved to be highly negative.

Emily finally left Washington perceiving this female reformer in the worst possible light; Myrtilla Miner acted peculiarly, was perhaps more biased than the hated slavocracy and exhibited capriciousness, selfishness and at times emotional instability. So, on the eve of the Civil War Emily Howland returned to Sherwood disillusioned with Myrtilla Miner, and undoubtedly with reformist activities and the role of the female reformer as well.

Once home, Emily quietly showed the depth of her loyalty to her mother, family and community. She assumed most of the domestic responsibilities of the household, giving her mother the care and attention she craved. Emily nursed her mother, visited with female friends and relatives in the vicinity of Sherwood, attended meetings for worship and business and traveled with the family on pleasure trips to western New York and once to Wisconsin. Giving her brother William's wife, Hannah, a needed rest from the household duties, Emily managed and directed the day help so that the washing, sewing, cleaning, cooking and gardening in and around the house progressed at an efficient pace. In comparison with the stimulating intellectual life in Philadelphia, and the physically and spiritually exhausting experiences in Washington, life in this closed rural community may have been very difficult for Emily to bear. Her letters indicate that it fed neither her intellect nor her reformist appetite fully but satisfied other needs—being loved and loving, security, a sense of belonging and being needed.

Emily felt most alive when reading and writing, which occupied an increasingly large portion of her day. The pen became her medium of expression since she felt that she could use it with more freedom and thought than the tongue. The twin solitary pursuits of reading and writing, with thought as the bridge between them, became the core of her existence during the next three years.

Her journal entries became increasingly longer in length and appear more frequently. Her correspondence, prodigious at all times, similarly increased so that a substantial portion of her day must have been spent alone at her desk composing these letters and entries.

In this lonely turning inward Howland seems initially to have found neither depression nor despair but an option to her existence in Sherwood and she discovered certain facets of her own personality never before faced. It is as though the ideas and values laid before her by the Philadelphia group during that decade were seeds that had been planted in Emily's mind. They had gradually germinated in the warm, supportive atmosphere of Philadelphia and then Washington. Now, in Sherwood, they began to blossom forth into mature and integrated value and belief systems. In removing herself from the immediate reformist task of teaching in Washington, Emily had provided herself with the opportunity to further examine the more general realm of feminist and reformist meanings and values. She could now turn to the pursuit of the intellectual by using "the critical, creative and contemplative side of the mind."

Her concern with the core values of society emerge most strongly from the pages of her journal. There she pondered the future course of the antislavery movement and, more personally, the problem of being a woman in nineteenth century America. In these journals she

also left a record of her reactions ranging from face to face encounters on the most mundane level to prominent events taking
place on the national stage at the outbreak of the Civil War.

Emily paradoxically had embraced feminism without coming to
terms with her own womanhood. Her journal during these three
years reveals her attempts to view herself as a woman and to better
define her unusual position within society at large. In the late 1840s
she had rejected the idea of entering into a traditional marriage but
never gave the reasons for the decision. Perhaps she felt that
marriage would be incompatible with her emerging feminist striving
for autonomy and equality. What is clear is that Howland chose not
to spend the traditional courtship years at balls and teas in search of
a husband but to spend her time for the most part in Philadelphia,
emotionally closed to male advances and open and dependent upon
the members of the Philadelphia female network. Nor did her parents urge her to marry; perhaps both Slocum and Hannah in their
own ways were at times seductive toward Emily wanting her in
Sherwood with them rather than married.

Returning home in 1859, Emily felt the need to clarify her unusual marital status—a position which would appear more deviant
among her friends and relatives in New York than among her Philadelphia friends.

> There are two classes of women, the strong minded and the
> weak. Among these are varying species, but one type. One rides
> the top wave of society, is the pampered doll of fashion. She has
> privileges and adulation and is satisfied. The other species of
> those who have no rights and want none, are the drudges.
> These of course are the large majority. Like the plantation
> slaves, hard work crushes out all aspirations. They have no
> time to think. Their contentment is despair. Among the strong
> minded, we find a large majority who wish their rights, who fret
> in the strait jacket, but dread the odium and loss of men's ad-
> miration more than they love principle. These will laugh over
> strong minded women, while ready to walk in every path their
> bleeding feet have made smooth and safe.
>
> Lastly are the brave women who fling off the cankering load
> to vanity, and armed with the panoply of truth fight the battle
> of freedom for their sex.

Emily leaves little doubt as to which species she wished to be counted among though she clearly considered the costs of such a choice. With her decision to teach in Washington, she had rejected her birthright membership in the privileged leisure class. The decision not to marry which she made in her early twenties ruled out placing her in a position she considered analogous to the slave—that of a conventionally married woman with no rights. One of her greatest fears was the loss of her precious freedom to read and write and, of course, to think. An alliance with those men she had met up to this time would have meant a partial loss of this freedom, a sacrifice Howland was not ready to make. Dating from her teenage years when she petitioned the politicians in her community, Emily displayed a refreshing indifference to what her male contemporaries thought of her dress, behavior or opinions. Certainly her father's mode of childrearing had not conditioned Emily to expect or seek the overt approval of any man.

That this attitude made certain of her friends and relatives clearly uneasy was demonstrated in their obvious desire to understand, or at least to rationalize, why she was not yet married. One of the more persistent was her cousin Rebecca Tallcot who, in an amusing series of letters, attempted to highlight the advantages of "old maidism." In an effort to console Emily, who appears not to have needed an ounce of consolation, Rebecca Tallcot only succeeded in expressing her own belief that being unmarried by choice was deviant and suspect, to say the very least. Her typical letter would begin with the statement that "boys should marry . . . nothing like it to settle and fix good habits and sound character. What is a man without a wife— a mere 0." The next remarks would make one believe that Emily had found a sympathetic feminist relative; Rebecca would extoll the female "left free from *entangling alliances*" for "they can more easily strike off and make their mark." But the next sentence would usually dispel this illusion—Rebecca would remind Emily that she expected yet "to see thee the happy wife of some clever man." Eventually such queries and discussions tapered off.

Less amusing to her family and the community of Orthodox Friends was Emily's deviance from the strictures of the Society. At one point when questioned by an aunt about her approval of dancing and music, Emily felt it was necessary to first draft a reply in her journal before answering in writing to her aunt. In a well-reasoned essay she exhibited an ecumenical attitude, rejecting the strict sectarian approach inherent in the Orthodox community's childrearing practices.

"I too most heartily condemn late hours, extravagance and unhealthy dressing and always use my influence against them. But in my view this (dancing) is as innocent a form of physical exercise and recreation as jumping rope." Howland had begun with a general discussion of forbidden amusements but quickly warmed to the central point of this exchange of views. "Truth compels me to say that nowhere have I witnessed such a distance, such a wall between youth and maturity as among Friends . . . It is fear, perpetual fear of espionage and censure. Is not love a safer principle by which to guide them, even tho — to gain it some cherished scruples have to be overlooked? Youth is irrepressible, it comes but once in life, it must do some frolicking, let age curb it within the bounds of reason, not try to stifle it. We cannot honor our predecessors by mechanically imitating them. We only truly follow them when we show the same earnestness to do our duty in our time with our convictions that they did in theirs."

Paradoxically, Emily did not strive to change her fellow Friends' sectarian attitudes although she strongly disagreed with the direction her Orthodox Friends had taken. She increasingly stayed away from the Society's meetings for business and worship, and let her preference for the social activism and less sectarian attitude of the Unitarians be known. Yet, she continued to retain her membership in the monthly meeting. She may have done this out of a concern for her mother, fearing that an outright break with the meeting would hurt Hannah deeply. Emily herself may not have understood fully the complexity of her motivations in this matter for she wrote at this time that spiritually "verily I am still a riddle to myself." As a Friend she felt she must tolerate and attempt to understand the position taken by her fellow members. When she realized that her position was incompatible with that of the majority of members, she began to withdraw from their midst. She nevertheless felt firmly that she must "not allow the molehill of petty things to become a mountain hiding from view God's own light of a glorious opportunity to help his cause." Therefore she would struggle alone if necessary to carry out her duties to help God's cause without expecting or receiving the support and fellowship of her monthly meeting.

As the fateful spring of 1861 approached Emily, much like the nation, was entering into "one of those seasons of horror that reveal my darkest self to myself." She no longer considered herself to be walking the high road of duty, transfigured and unsoiled by the dust of common things. The longer she remained in Sherwood the more she was pulled "down, down into the mire out of which I toiled and here as now I wallow. It is long since I have been thus tossed. God grant that this may be the last and triumphant contest. I stand before myself a poor, vain weakling, I who felt so strong, so sure I had taken my position and could stand upon it."

She had chosen to return to Sherwood and was now realizing the tragic consequences of that action. Isolated from her Philadelphia network and their loving intellectual and moral support, Emily had mistakenly assumed that the pen could substitute for these primary relationships. She thought that her correspondence and journals would adequately bridge the two worlds in which she wished to live. Instead she found herself neither an active member of an intellectual community servicing blacks and women nor leading a contented life of Quakerly domesticity in Sherwood.

Emily Howland at no time clearly delineated her motives for continuing to remain in Sherwood. Her decision to stay at her parents' home during these years may have stemmed from a twofold consideration: her continuing indecisiveness regarding the costs as well as the rewards of embracing the female reformer's role, and the guilt she experienced for wishing to abandon her familial and domestic responsibilities. Although Emily was unhappy, and at times depressed while living in Sherwood she nevertheless was not ready to enter reformist work elsewhere.

In her journal during the winter of 1861, she recorded a bout with what she termed "her darkest self." In a rather unique stylistic form Emily wrote a forceful deeply introspective conversation, one which is hard to believe was meant (as she noted) for no other eyes than hers. The first voice in this conversation is Emily speaking as feminist, reformer and intellectual. The second is Emily as the traditional maternal-domestic woman embodied in the character she labeled Earth.

The first voice, belonging to the intellectual-reformer states definitively:

> I have found my place and I feel sure it is the right one.

And Earth responded:

> Why then do you have to pit yourself against your pitiless logic to convince yourself of a self-evident truth? You take the position of single woman voluntarily, why falter at the consequences, why care for slights, for lack of caste and place or be chilled by isolation, are you not with the right, if you've got it stronger than the slighters?

Earth's attack continued unmercifully.

> Are you sure you are not living a mistake? I, Earth, teach you in every lesson I give, in plastic matter, that isolation is wrong. Marriage is the law. She who rebels must feel the edge of the waves, if her little barque be not utterly swept out of sight on the ocean of life. Do they cut? I am glad of it. Be willing to bow your neck to my yoke, meekly, when you've suffered enough, where you would once have distained to bow it. It has been done many a time by a prouder spirit than yours.

But Emily-as-feminist interrupts this archetypal Earth-Mother's soliloquy with this appeal:

> Here I raise my hand and beg for a word in self defense, before I am swept away. I am not proud, I only mean to live as truly and freely as I can, and in thus doing strengthen my weak sisters to the same. With all deference to the Earth in its place, I believe in a Higher Power with my whole soul.

And then from the depths of Emily's being this cry, radical and timeless in content, eloquence and sincerity, is heard.

> I do not hate Earth its pleasures, its fashions or its peoples, but if they cast me off because I do not make them the end of life, if they scorn me because I will not follow them wholly, then welcome isolation. Never shall any amount of suffering of the earthy slough off the divine. Let the sensitive and vain suffer and perish and fall away. They will leave scars on the poor soul, these I dread but they are better than the rank branches and blooms of earthliness. It is terrible to be alone, it makes the earthling shiver, but is not the sea alone in its mightiness, is not God alone, are not they harmonious, each, and with the Uni-

verse too? Then cannot the human soul be great, true, pure, free alone? Yes, I know it. I feel it, I exalt in it, but alas I am so human, my vanity makes me suffer so, when I see myself passed by because forsooth I am a cipher in the world's esteem if I lack the initial figure of a man at my left. O Earth, I loathe you for these distortions, for this injustice which meets and baffles me at every step. I sometimes long for the blindness which possesses my poor sex, but never can I hide my eyes from seeing, tho to see is agony.
One proof after another rolls in upon me, a mountain of wrongs crushing down the poor little woman. Is she like the spring in the mountain strong enough to burst it asunder and rise up a soul emancipate? The human eye says "no, this must be the place designed for you, see you can't make out anything." The eye of faith says. "Yes soul is stronger than earth, all the fashions, all the seeming comliness thereof come to do it reverence, it shall yet subdue all matter to its service."

Emily's world was a fearful one, fraught with dangers, loneliness and, most appalling to her, lack of freedom and justice. She felt that her perception of the world was far different from that of her non-feminist sisters and, in turn, far more disturbing. As a member of a female reformer-intellectual network, she had been exposed to their view of the world and had now incorporated the main body of their ideology into her belief system. More important, although she saw political and social injustice, Emily perceived and perhaps feared the increased conflict fighting against such injustice would bring into her life; her ambivalent position in Sherwood stemmed in large part from this uncomfortable dualistic world view.

Emily throughout this experience however had not lost a sense of hope for the resolution of this inequity to her sex. Although this hope made her agonizing perception of the world more bearable, during these years she did not feel that she had the strength to act decisively on the emerging conflicts in her own life, no matter how strong her determination to crusade for change.

Her actions proved to be far more hesitant and far less radical than her words in doing battle for her sex. In fact, her reformist concerns during these years, were centered on abolitionist activities rather than overtly feminist works. An anguished entry in her journal on December 2, 1859, the day of John Brown's death, heralds her preoccupation with the fate of Southern blacks. She captured the abolitionist spirit of that day and recorded it for those of another century to read.

> Today is ever memorable in our history yes in the world. Today is a great speck in the revolution thro which we pass. Today Virginia says to the man who its governor (Wise) styles the best and bravest man he ever saw, 'Mount the scaffold, the scaffold I have built for you and die. You shall not live, your goodness your bravery, we fear.' Wo! Wo! Wo! is surely to come upon all the fair-seeming of this land. Is the measure of our transgressions full or lacketh it yet a little? Who shall see and on whom shall it fall to act what is to come? Who will be the cowards and who the brave? This is my prophecy that men will fight for the right before they will vote for it. There will probably be a dissolution of the Union before ever a republican president is elected.
>
> There is a straight to the point action about fighting that does not entangle small minds and befog them as political schisms and schemes do.

Historians of this century are divided in evaluating the effects of abolitionism in the sectional crisis; particularly controversial is the role it played as a cause of the Civil War. One interpretation of the reaction of Northern abolitionists to and the consequence of John Brown's raid on Harper's Ferry and his subsequent death in 1859, is unusually fruitful in understanding Emily's record of the second of December. It has been suggested that the Harper's Ferry crisis was one of means not ends if one examines the questions John Brown's actions raised about the method of attaining the goal of abolition. By this date Howland had internalized the idealization of John Brown as a symbol of the moral order and the social purpose of the Northern cause. By joining with those apotheosizing Brown, she had implicitly rejected the principle that differences should be settled by ballots not bullets, thus compromising the Quaker means of achieving abolition, the creed of nonviolence.

Taking her place with the extremists of the movement Emily saw nothing illogical about her intellectual abandonment of pacifism. If a militant stance was necessary to align oneself with the oppressed rather than with the oppressor, then Howland had no qualms in choosing such a position.

In Emily the crisis psychology precipitated by the death of John
Brown continued and deepened throughout the next year, mirroring
the fear of impending disaster flourishing throughout the North and
South. This fear was realized when the first Northern and Southern
shots were exchanged at Fort Sumter and with the Northern occupation of the Sea Islands around Beaufort, South Carolina. With the
advent of the Civil War in April, 1861, Emily's martial spirit
appears to have been aroused. Although she had written about the
battle for freedom for women, she chose to fight for the freedom of
the blacks. She and Anna Searing offered their services to the Reverend Samuel J. May to join "Gideon's Band" and teach in the Sea
Islands. Perhaps Emily felt that this would prove more acceptable to
her family than overt feminist activity and additionally was in har-
mony with her intention to "contribute to the cause of the forlorn
even if it be teaching those to whom knowledge had been denied."

As the full extent and intensity of the war became better understood by both North and South during late 1861 and 1862, Emily
received letters from friends in Washington telling of political and
military developments in that city. When in late 1862 letters
included accounts of the plight of black women and children sent in
from the Virginia front as the Union Army advanced that fall, Emily
abruptly decided not to venture into the chaotic situation in the Sea
Islands with Anna Searing. Instead, she opted to return to the familiar environs of Washington to work in what was called Contraband
Camp which had been established in the fall of 1862 inside the city
limits. There she could work doing a service that would give her a
measure of dignity, respect and independence which was lacking in
her life in the village. A secondary advantage would be the return to
her circle of friends, the Danas, Bowens, and Breeds particularly,
who could provide her with a respite from her duties and encouragement and support for feminist as well as abolitionist beliefs.

Emily had not yet resolved many of the problems associated with
being both a single woman and a feminist, as well as her desire to be
an abolitionist reformer and intellectual in nineteenth century
America. But during her three years at home she had grown to
better understand and accept herself as an unusual woman. The ex-
pansion in the number of socially acceptable roles for women
created by wartime conditions helped her to refuse to be "a little
barque swept out of sight on the ocean of life." No longer passive,

aided by this national crisis, Emily asserted her right to be "a cinder in the eye to the world." She returned to Washington, well aware of the unpopular stance she had previously taken, and looked forward to the more socially acceptable role she was to take on as comforter to the contraband. A single woman by choice, a feminist by conviction, she had decided to work with the contrabands with whom she most closely identified for reasons which seemed more implicitly feminist than spiritual. Hardly motivated by the missionary and evangelical zeal of the Sea Islands teachers, Emily saw her decision as based on the commonality of her position with the contrabands— both she and they were people without status, lacking caste or place, chilled by isolation, alone and not truly free. She earnestly entered the contrabands' misery, quietly maintaining a belief that in thus doing she had at last begun to fight against that monstrous injustice that met and baffled her at every step. The double-edged sword of abolitionism and feminism, conceived by the Philadelphia group years earlier, could be grasped and used to free both blacks and women from their bondage.

4

Adversity: The Washington-Virginia Experiment

In late 1862, on the outskirts of the city of Washington, there were some twelve hundred black men, women and children living in converted cavalry stables built around a square which enclosed approximately an acre of ground. They were the inhabitants of one section of Contraband Camp. Over the past year women and children in addition to old and infirmed males had been sent here mainly from Fortress Monroe, General Benjamin F. Butler's command post in Virginia. Since the summer of 1861, when in a political declaration Butler announced slaves to be henceforth "contraband of war," they had streamed toward the Union Army in Virginia requesting refugee status. Being placed in the Washington camp these people for over a year knew neither slavery nor freedom but, as the word "contraband" connoted, were the highly questionable property of the Federal authorities.

President Lincoln on September 22, 1862 announced the preliminary emancipation proclamation, declaring all slaves held in parts of the United States not in the possession of the Union Army to be free as of January 1, 1863. After this date, these freedmen would also have the opportunity to receive wages by entering the army for garrison duty. With this proclamation the Federal government had taken a very crucial ideological step. The proclamation which in actuality freed no slaves did manage to have extensive political and military ramifications. With this declaration to abolish slavery the North was no longer waging war to preserve the Union but was now

51

fighting a war for freedom. This ideological step additionally recognized and intensified the ambiguity of the blacks' position in both the North and South.

Emily Howland arrived at Contraband Camp in the midst of this upheaval. Events taking place in this and other camps and freedman villages in which Emily worked, nursed and taught over the next four years pointed to myriad difficulties that were to be found on this road to emancipation. There was a glaring lack of organization, direction or concerted effort to systemically understand and deal with the needs of countless numbers of blacks under Federal control during the years 1863 to 1868. More important this haphazard approach was shared by both well-meaning friends of the blacks and those less charitably disposed. Unfortunately throughout postwar reconstruction it proved to be a model of white relations with freed blacks.

When Emily Howland entered Contraband Camp in early January of 1863 she recoiled from the sight meeting her gaze. Nothing in her previous experience had prepared her for the misery and suffering she witnessed before her. Smallpox, tuberculosis, pneumonia and pleurisy were prevalent in camp, afflicting the aged of both sexes as well as the young children. The roofs of stables and makeshift tents leaked, floors were constantly muddy and to compound the already existing unsanitary conditions, heat and clean bedding were not available. When it rained saturated clothes and bedding typically resulted, adding to the wretchedness of those under Federal care.

Surveying this situation, Emily realized that trying to teach inhabitants in the camp would be ludicrous until certain basic survival needs of the contrabands had been met. On her initial visits to the camp, she was accompanied by her old friend, Dr. Breed, now Assistant Surgeon at one of the Contraband Camp hospitals. Even though Emily had long been fascinated with the study of medicine, she decided to forego the role of nurse at the hospital, leaving this task to a young woman who had recently written to her begging "to do anything in the way of nursing." This letter marked the beginning of the lifelong friendship between Emily Howland and one of the best known of the Civil War nurses, Cornelia Hancock. It also marks the entrance of Cornelia Hancock into the Philadelphia network in which she was recognized as a fellow reformer, intellectual and friend.

Emily, not finding a nursing or teaching role acceptable to her, created a position in which she could best use her own talents and serve the needs of those in a newly formed section of the already overcrowded Washington Contraband Camp. This section, designated by the army as Camp Barker and under the military command of Captain James Ferree, had neither adequate housing nor medical facilities for newly arrived tidewater Virginia blacks. Seeing this need, Howland threw herself into organizational efforts. She wrote letters begging or cajoling contributions on behalf of freedmen to New York, Boston and Philadelphia freedmen's aid associations. Not satisfied with this she then sent messages to friends and relatives describing the lack of clothing, bandages, food, straw for bedding, soap, candles and sewing equipment in Camp Barker. She told various missionary societies, including the Philadelphia Friends Association and American Missionary Association how physical needs of the blacks must first be met before their spiritual and intellectual needs could be tackled. Within a month the first barrels and boxes began arriving for distribution, containing requested clothes, bedding, scraps of materials and edibles. Not surprisingly some female friends arrived from New York and Philadelphia to help with distribution of the goods. Typical was Mary Searing, Anna's sister and Emily's neighbor, who accompanied some material from Cayuga County and offered to help in whatever capacity possible.

Confusion over the direction and flow of authority within the camp was a continuing problem for the white caretakers. There were military and civilian overseers and medical personnel, missionaries and agents from benevolent freedmen associations and a small number of philanthropic individuals not affiliated with any of the government, military or relief organizations. No bureaucratic structure existed for Camp Barker, the contraband camps or for freedmen's villages in general. They comprised a unique and unprecedented response to General Butler's political actions at Fortress Monroe. Although the government had been dealing with a contraband situation in the Sea Islands in South Carolina since 1861, the complexities of the problems involving the contrabands around the capital were far different from those in the Sea Islands' "Port Royal Experiment."

In the Sea Islands economics, specifically the desire by Northerners to obtain a cotton profit, played an important role in structuring military and government agents relationship with the blacks; possession of land, growing of crops and cotton profit were problems to be dealt with. In Washington this was not the case; the contrabands were displaced people, having neither land to work nor profit to make for their white caretakers. Missionaries and teachers who arrived in Washington faced a different set of problems than those who journeyed to Port Royal. As Emily reiterated countless times during her first year in Washington, the Virginia contrabands desperately needed physical care to ward off starvation and disease. In sharp contrast with the Port Royal Experiment teaching and religious education played minor, if not non-existent, roles during the first year of the Washington camps' operation.

Emily Howland noted that the rules governing the white caretakers' behavior toward blacks and with each other were being made as each new situation arose. She came to Washington at a time when a society that had eschewed government bureaucracies and had depended steadfastly on religiously-oriented volunteerism was forced by the contingencies of war to deal with problems only a centrally organized bureaucracy could handle efficiently. She thus participated in an important stage of America's move towards a modern form of government. Her experiences would find echoes in the efforts of liberal reformers in the Washingtons of 1917, 1933 and 1942.

Emily solicited food, clothing, and personnel because she saw a need for these but was unsure of the response such actions would bring from both the camp's government agent and military leader. The relief associations were equally uncertain, judging by their letters to Emily, about the number, duties and responsibilities of their personnel to be sent to the camp. She was left on her own by military and government agents at Camp Barker to devise a method of distributing the material which she had solicited, and to deal with the blacks as she saw fit.

February, 1863 found Emily at the camp six days a week, from ten in the morning until sunset. In the company of Mary Searing and Carrie Nichols, the wife of the Assistant Superintendent of the camp, she visited the black people, ascertaining their needs, distributing clothing and aiding those women healthy enough to work with their sewing and mending. But the situation at Camp Barker soon exasperated her; new arrivals were constantly adding to the chaos—it was apparent that there was no end to the need. There were three hospitals for the sick but many preferred to remain in their own makeshift homes. Tending the sick and dying, making their last hours less lonely and painful, Emily began to gain a new and different perspective of the newly freed people. Although her understanding of those in her care was far from complete, she realized the source of their new-found dignity and respected their right to choose how and where they would spend those last hours before death.

She requested permission to remain at the camp overnight, a practice not observed by the other eight white civilians in her section. The consternation this request aroused is evident by the sudden flurry of letters from friends in Philadelphia and New York, and particularly from her family. Even among that circle of Christian abolitionist women who had influenced her to enter such work, this request drew some strong criticism. None but Emily saw the ironic discrepancy between their espousal of the equality of all persons and their hesitation to act in ways other than paternal. It was one thing to distribute clothing and food by day at the camp but to live among "the culled pusson," never to escape this environment to "breathe a purer atmosphere and have different influences" was unthinkable to even the more ardent antislavery advocates. In the end, Emily acquiesced and went to live with Mary Searing's cousin near the camp.

Emily herself was not altogether free from the less overt racial and class prejudices of her era. More than once she coyly imitated black speech and idioms in her letters and journal and with a sense of superiority discussed certain aspects of the freedmen's behavior as quaint, barbaric or stereotypically childlike. Her incredulous reaction when she witnessed her first "shout," a bodyswaying dance that followed praying and singing of spirituals, was not unlike the reaction of her female philanthropic counterparts in the Sea Islands. A group of new black arrivals to the camp were obliged to go to bed supperless; to Emily they appeared "happy." Later some of them collected in the yard, singing words of "the foolishest kind," clapping and swaying their bodies. "It was a strange barbarous scene. You might have thought yourself in Central Africa." Years later, having watched countless such gatherings, Emily remained amazed and disconcerted by such "African" and almost pagan practices.

Emily also slipped comfortably into the habit of calling older men and women "uncles" and "aunties" and the younger women and men "girls" and "boys." They in turn referred to her as "Miss Emily," a term, incidentally, by which she preferred to be addressed by all but her very closest friends in years to come. The next step in her relationship with camp freedmen was not unusual; she became possessive. By midsummer camp people were now "her people," older women were "her dear old Aunties," and she began to ask for aid and comfort for "her poor, precious 'contrabands'." With pride she looked on as twenty black men in her area enlisted in the army, making her feel that "in the hour of our dispair (sic) light comes from the dark places."

Although the number in camp was constantly fluctuating, certain families remained at Camp Barker and to these Emily was particularly drawn. Since teaching at Miner's school, she had been involved in placing young black acquaintances in wealthy white homes in New York, New Jersey and Philadelphia. These children were educated and/or taught a trade in exchange for work in the house or place of business. She now began to beseech her wealthy contacts in these three areas to take an increasing number of young girls and boys. Her evenings away from camp were filled with sending lengthy messages of appreciation for goods sent, appeals for more clothing and food, and placing willing contrabands in available homes with wealthy families.

Emily sincerely wished to help the blacks for whom she had taken responsibility in the Washington camp. Not surprisingly though, she did feel a sense of superiority and dominance over these people. She had journeyed to Washington to live with the freedmen with whom she identified so closely. Once there however this sense of identification was no longer evident. Emily had stepped from a socially unacceptable, powerless role into one which allowed her greater freedom, authority and respect than ever before. She had become one of the white caretakers and in stepping into this position of power distanced herself emotionally from the black people around her.

At the same time that she was exploring her changing feelings toward contrabands, she was becoming increasingly frustrated and disillusioned with inefficiency and poor management of various benevolent associations. She wrote to the Philadelphia, Boston and New York religious associations recommending a small school be established since young children were now in a better position to benefit from some education. "The American Tract Society, as if to atone for its past misdeeds toward this people, had builded (sic) a neat little house for meetings and school just outside the camps. Yesterday came the teacher, a young man who had taught among them. Contrary to my expectations, he asked Mary and myself to join him, so we have very short schools morning and after noon, soon they are to be held in the evening for adults."

Emily was perhaps unduly harsh in criticizing the efforts of freedmen's relief associations for they were as ignorant of their rights and duties with contraband camps as was she at an earlier date. With no clearcut chain of command evident to newly recruited benevolent association employees on their arrival in Washington, it is possible to see how these camp philanthropists, missionaries and teachers failed to work cooperatively in many instances.

Emily continued with her duties at camp through the summer and fall before seeking relief and relaxation in a visit to Philadelphia. But while visiting with her Philadelphia female friends in November, she received word that efficient functioning in her camp had broken down with her departure. A substitute for Emily in the distribution room, although well-meaning, had offended and wounded the feelings of applicants, so that now the people were secretly taking clothes at night in lieu of having to listen to the substitute's lecture on their character and morals. When Emily returned to "her people" shortly thereafter, the scene was one of happiness for all. "Rode up in most jolting style in a market wagon. Such a burst of welcome greeted me from a half dozen children who descried me in the dark as brot many of larger growth, who all nearly smothered me with rejoiceings (sic) and made me feel very happy, forgetful of weariness or any down in the mouth feeling."

Meanwhile, new orders governing camps inhabitants had arrived. A small number of men, women and children were to be sent to the confiscated Arlington estate of General Robert Lee to garden corn and vegetables for the contraband for fall and winter use. Emily failed to interpret this action correctly as the permanent removal of blacks from the capital camps to an economically more self-sufficient colony still under government control. Instead she imagined that her contraband camp people would become the first loyal Union owners of General Lee's domain.

The experiment in Arlington soon proved successful enough for the Bureau of Refugees, Freedmen and Abandoned Lands to decide to settle the occupants from Camp Barker permanently in a village on the Arlington estate. The new chapel was dedicated the first week of December and by the middle of the month the majority of people had been moved across the river. Camp Barker was officially closed on December 21, 1863 but not before acrimony erupted among the bureau officials, military officers and civilian workers. Emily, following Army orders, remained a few more days after this packing up "amidst heaps of ruins and rats," due to the "great uncertainty of all things connected with the military system." She was anxious to move across the Potomac to help settle the older people in a special home. "There is a great deal there to be done. I greatly desire to go there when I can have a place to myself, but I must wait until way opens. Nichols (Asst. Supt.) is very jealous of his power and harrasses and torments and thwarts all he can, but (a) way may open, meantime I shall bide my time and make myself very busy among those left behind."

The new year found Emily at Camp Todd, Virginia, as the Arlington estate was officially renamed. For once given proper

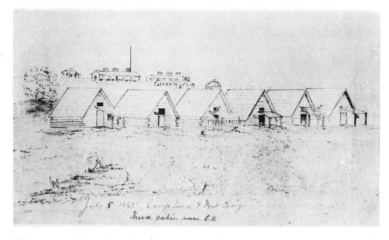

The teachers' quarters where Emily lived part of the time while teaching at the Freedmen's school, Camp Todd (Arlington) Virginia. Pencil sketch by Emily Howland, 1865. (Courtesy Friends Historical Library of Swarthmore College)

authority to act decisively, by the military leader Captain James Ferree, she had a log room added to the school house so that sixty day pupils and those adults in the evening school could be properly accommodated. This action did not endear her to Mr. Nichols; she was supplied with rations of wood but none of food. "That devolves upon Nichols (now Supt.) and he considers me inimical to his interests which certainly I am as far as in my power."

These antagonistic feelings between federal administrator and educator were to be reenacted in scenes in freedmen villages and throughout the South during Reconstruction. An interesting contrast can be drawn between events taking place in that other experiment, the Sea Islands, and at the Washington-Virginia camps. The military, missionaries and teachers at Camp Barker, and later at Camp Todd, stood in grudging unity against those civilians representing federal bureaus from 1862 to 1864; they did not display the series of shifting alliances among military, federal and civilian workers as was the case in the Sea Islands. Although complaints against the military were frequent enough, the missionaries and educators in the Washington area did not consider their differences with them to be one of goals but only means. But such was not the case with the Bureau superintendent. Few letters were exchanged among Emily's camp associates that did not include some mention of the cruelty, evilness or power-driven characteristics of the reigning non-military superintendent. They viewed the Bureau as standing in clear opposition to their goals of educating freedmen so that they might be better able to cope in the new world of freedom after the war.

Many military officers assigned to Camp Barker and Camp Todd were avid abolitionists from New York and Massachusetts. Although they found themselves at times defending an unpopular government policy regulating the mobility of camp inhabitants when military action drew near, these same officers expressed their continued sympathy with educational and religious goals of missionaries and teachers within the camp. The camp superintendent, on the other hand, was concerned only with efficient and inexpensive management of the camp. Federal food, clothing and wood rations, garden crop success or failure and the size and number of people within his district were matters of primary importance. Emily noted many times that the number of men, women and children would fluctuate constantly so that an accurate record upon which to base rationing estimates was not available to the superintendent. However, Emily felt that Bureau superintendents were more concerned with these matters than with the spiritual and moral welfare of blacks. Such sentiments were expressed by other female philanthropists working with freedmen and Bureau superintendents during the Civil War. Laura Towne in the Sea Islands during this period complained that superintendents forced black men "to prove they are fit to be free by holding a tyrant's power over them," exhibiting "narrowness on the subject of antislavery."

Emily's world was not an experiment championed by Congresspeople and members of the Cabinet as was the Sea Island Experiment. Neither was it viewed as the proving ground for freedmen; rather the Washington-Virginia contraband camps and freedmen villages can be seen as unplanned, unsponsored responses to the exigencies of black tidewater Virginians, displaced without status and identity by the Civil War. The military, missionaries and teachers in the Washington-Virginia area appear to have cooperated with one another to ensure their own safety as well as the safety and education of freedmen under their care. Bureau officials, although living in close proximity to other white caretakers, did not share in this fellowship. Unfortunately, we will never know whether blacks, over whom the controversies raged, perceived the division of duties, responsibilities and motives among their white caretakers in the same manner.

The military, missionaries and teachers were living under unusual circumstances in Camp Todd by the spring of 1863. Their sympathetic mutual interest in freedmen and their antipathy for Bureau officials, as well as the danger associated with the proximity of war, can all be considered factors in the quick formation of many strong friendships that developed among these white caretakers. Social etiquette was discarded and many rules governing sex role behavior were less stringently followed. Females were no longer chaperoned, escorted and pampered; in more than one case women were allowed the same mobility, rights and responsibilities as their fellow male teachers and missionaries. Emily was expected to walk the same five mile distance daily to canvass camps as her companion Reverend Johnson; Lizzie Bailey was required to run Bailey's Farm and take courier duty to Washington from Camp Todd as well as her philanthropically-motivated brother Jonathan; Caroline Putnam could travel to Washington unescorted without causing raised eyebrows while Mrs. Isaac Wister followed her surgeon husband from camp to camp caring for wounded soldiers.

This freedom from stereotyped role expectations may have contributed to the emergence of one relationship in particular. Captain James Ferree, the military leader at Camps Barker and Todd, appears to have been held in high regard by teachers and missionaries at both camps. Courteous, well-educated and committed to the education of contrabands in his care Ferree used his position to implement the plans of educators and missionaries, sometimes directly contradicting the wishes of camp overseers from the Bureau. His attention was more frequently than not directed toward Emily Howland during much of 1863 and 1864. Ferree escorted her personally to the city and obtained special privileges for her. He also helped to make her life at camp more tolerable since she now lived there with her fellow philanthropists. That they were attracted to one another is evident from the references to them in their mutual friends' correspondence at this time. Strangely enough, in sharp contrast to these letters, Emily at no time in the existing letters and journals mentioned Ferree except in terms of his official position with the camp. If she thought of Ferree in terms other than friendship, it was neither recorded nor saved. By mid-1865 his name is seldom mentioned in her correspondence with one exception. She described an encounter in which he sought her advice regarding marriage. She told him of the negative view toward marriage that she continued to hold for herself and suggested maternally that he enter that state after only the greatest caution and deliberation. Ferree rejected her advice summarily, entered shortly thereafter into an unhappy marriage, and regretted it almost immediately. She apparently did not appeal for advice to her Philadelphia female network on this subject. In fact, she exhibited surprising strength in not seeking their support for her position. Their camp friends however considered her decision not to marry unfathomable and viewed Ferree's marriage as a retaliatory action. One well-meaning friend managed to invest the situation with an undue note of tragedy and told Emily after Ferree's marriage, "Poor child. His eager questioning about thee showed where his heart is. How I pity him." Almost twenty years later, Ferree resumed correspondence with Emily expressing his unchanging admiration of and devotion to her. Unfortunately, she again left no record of her reaction to these rather remarkable letters. Pity, regret, admiration or love—if these emotions were felt, it will never be known.

Another close friendship sprang up between Emily and two missionaries, Reverend and Mrs. Johnson. J. R. Johnson was a tall, gangly man, as awkward in his relationships with other people as he was in his own motions. Unaffiliated with any church, missionary or freedmen's association, Johnson arrived at the Washington camp armed only with determination to work among blacks in whatever capacity his God found for him. Impractical to an extreme he left cares of everyday life, including a lack of income, to his wife while he pursued his other-worldly concerns. Emily was immediately endeared to this couple for their selfless motivation to aid freedmen and she took them under wing, finding support for him among various associates and bailing them out financially on more than one occasion.

When her duties at Camp Todd had settled down into a fairly comfortable routine, Emily and Reverend Johnson decided to visit some of the new neighboring black settlements that were not under aid or protection of Camp Todd. Out of this visit Emily's "circuit" evolved. On their initial visit they were surprised to find a number of small communities existing in poverty that managed to overshadow even the pressing needs of their more fortunate brethren inside government lines. Emily and Johnson picked out five settlements that appeared to be in the greatest need of medical supplies, food, clothing and direction.

Emily once again began to write to her friends within benevolent societies, requesting donations specifically for these settlements. The National Freedman's Association in New York responded by engaging her as teaching supervisor of a district covering these settlements, by hiring the necessary number of teachers and by making J. R. Johnson an unofficial general agent of the project. Before this plan could be put into action, however, the Bureau and the military agreed that for security purposes facilities for freedmen at Camp Todd be dismantled and camp people relocated once again, this time on Mason's Island in the Potomac River northwest of Washington, immediately opposite Georgetown. Discouraged Emily did not turn to her Philadelphia group for help since most members were in-

volved in geographically separate activities. Instead, she returned to
Sherwood for a brief visit with her family and returned with Anna
Searing in tow to help teach on Mason's Island.

Emily found the island a place of great beauty and comfort when
compared with conditions she had previously lived under at Camp
Todd. At the southern end of the island a large residence stood
which was once the home of J. M. Mason, the "rebel" envoy to
Europe. "The apartments are spacious and lofty, the dancing salon
large and airy, the grounds beautiful, adorned with rare old trees. It
looks like a home to be happy in, but like Blue Beard's castle it holds
its horrors," Emily recounted. In a fashion characteristic of an avid
abolitionist, she went on dramatically to reveal that beneath those
pleasant rooms were "dungeons, worthy of feudal days, dungeons
dark and damp, where the lordly and brutal owners once immured
their human chattels when it suited their pleasure. But what poetic
justice, stranger than any romance, this revolution awards the
oppressor. That house is now occupied by the Supt. of Freedmen
here, that salon, once filled with merry music and tripping feet, is
now a school room where Quakeresses gather their sable pupils, the
children in the day, the parents in the evening! Here they are taught
what it was once a crime to teach them—how to read."

The days rolled by in rapid progression as Emily using Mason's
Island as the center of her activities, traveled to and taught in new
schools in the area. She felt that the four Quaker women under her
supervision were excellent teachers as well as good friends. Together
these women brought to their work an unswerving dedication to the
advancement of the freedmen and enjoyed sharing their uniquely
satisfying experiences. Adding to her contentment was the small
number of black families she had grown to know and love, in a
rather paternalistic manner, over the past two years. She had taught
them to read and write, furnished them with food and clothes when
necessary, and now was teaching them to be self sufficient. Having
supplied them with the necessary seeds and farming equipment at
Camp Todd, she had fought with Bureau officials so that the land
around·each shanty could be used for each family's private farming
needs.

Now with this newest relocation to the island she felt that these
families needed her more than ever. The frequent changes in
Federal jurisdiction and the overall lack of direction and policy had

taken its toll. Alliances among the four groups caring for the camp people began to shift after so many relocations and new superintendents. The militiary, Federal officials, teachers and missionaries, each frustrated by the lack of progress and results, were now in open and at times direct antagonism with one another. Two dollars a month ground rent was now required of all freedmen within government lines, there was no room for farming around the shanties on the island and the self sufficiency and independence Emily had been trying to foster was now in danger of being destroyed. Although most of her "old flock nested in around here, the rest have gone out and put up shanties in two different spots." The reason that they chose not to remain under governmental care was due to actions of the newest commander of the island, Captain Brown from Massachusetts. All children over ten or twelve years of age were ordered removed from their parents and bound out. When the Assistant Superintendent with four soldiers arrived to carry out the order, families that normally would have remained in camp fled the borders and built their makeshift homes outside government lines.

Emily felt obliged to continue her work with those she knew outside camp and added these little settlements to her growing circuit list. Although this humanitarian gesture stemmed from a genuine concern for these people, it also must be noted that it was not untouched by that sense of superiority into which she often slipped when speaking of the freedmen. "Those who are trying to take care of themselves will need more looking after in every respect," Emily told her mother. She continued to see freedmen, even those she had known intimately over the past two years, as simple, uncomplicated persons, childlike and dependent upon her in most respects. "They attribute all their tossings and misfortunes to my leaving them, now I suppose they anticipate a dawn of prosperity" she wrote to her father on a return to her base camp at Mason's Island.

The struggle between her responses to the blacks around her remained; but if paternalism was still prevalent, a deeper understanding of their behavior was slowly emerging. Although the "shout" continued to bother her, she understood the place music held in their lives and the function it served. Transported from place to place, cut loose from the bonds of their past, with no identity in the present and uncertainty looming as the main ingredient for the future, Emily saw that "this musical expression of their whole being is a necessity to them. It is this power of becoming absorbed and carried up for a time above their degradation, all their sorrows in the breath of song or of devotion, which has kept the souls and bodies of this trampled race alive." She thus found that "through their hearty love of the beautiful, the task of educating them for the dignity of freedom is made less wearisome, more hopeful."

Emily had no doubts but that she was educating them to lead lives as free men and women with full political, economic and social rights. She managed to ignore the controversy surrounding the disposition of freedmen if the North won the war. As in the old abolitionist days she unbendingly maintained the position she had chosen, refusing to acknowledge that other options less favorable to blacks might be chosen by those in power. She read and interpreted President Lincoln's second inaugural address to her people the first week in March, 1865. Her interpretation significantly revolved around the belief that these ex-slaves were shortly to gain those rights and responsibilities of free men.

One practice among the freedmen regarding rights and responsibilities disconcerted Emily—their failure to adopt a legal marriage ceremony once free from the bonds of slavery. In her adult classes she exhorted them to accept the responsibility of a legal marriage and even tied this into her interpretation of Lincoln's address. Secretly Emily found herself amused by the irony of her actions, a woman dedicated to remaining single engaged in wholeheartedly advocating the institution of marriage.

Emily in her youth rarely evidenced a sense of humor but since her arrival in Washington, she had begun to view and adroitly express her opinion of certain serio-comical facets of camp life. The delightful ability to gain a sense of proportion through humor and wit, to grasp a comical or ironic side of an untenable situation or action and to be able to laugh at herself and thus gain a new perspective had become trademarks of her personality. But one letter Emily wrote, on April 15, 1865, was completely devoid of all but the most desolate feelings.

> The greatest consternation is upon us all in this little community because of the shocking rumor that 'Uncle Sam' as the people call the president was murdered last night and also the Sec. of War. I was waked at a very early hour by a man coming

with the tale, when I put my head out of the door, the men were walking around in solemn groups, all appealed to me of course. All this fills me with a dread that it may be (true). I cannot hear and the anxiety is wearisome. What a very strange ending of the glorious week wherein peace dawned upon us! I see it is not impossible that this terrible tragedy may be that some desperado may have thus gratified his vengeance, but it seems very unreal, very weird, like a freak of a morbid imagination. But such a one might have wrought the dreadful deed!

The skies weep and a burden fills the air. The longer I dwell on it the more incredible it seems. It will be a great relief to know that it was a wild tale . . .

That horrid story, I cannot think of anything else. When I study the event taking it as a fact, I see that Lincoln's star has culminated, he had finished his great work or seen through, the whole nation trusts and revers him, 4,000,000 nearly worship him, the glorious time for him to die is now. He could never again be so much to us as he has been and now is. At no time in his after life would his memory be so precious, so sacred as now. I am sure something unusually dreadful had happened, all the rumors are the same.

The question is 'how can we do without him'!

My washer woman has just come in. She says she has been up to the fort and says the soldiers assure her the rumor is true. She said their breakfast was untasted and their commanding officer has hurried to the city to learn the truth.

Benjamin returned from the fort and says it is true. Our president is certainly murdered.

The air seems filled with sadness and forebodings or trouble. I do not feel like another word. One's brains reel under the blow. The air had seemed thick with gloom all day. I never felt anything like it before—the stillness like the held breath. No talking among the men, even of this talking people. They seem to feel fully their great calamity. We must live on.

1st day morning. One must go on living.

The shock, uncertainty, disbelief and finally despair that accompanied news of the first assassination of an American president would not be forgotten by Emily or her people. The day would be relived countless times in their lives—where they were, what they had been doing, the routine of their camp life suddenly broken never to be pieced together again in the same way. Emily's estimation of the President and his place in history will always be open to argument; but when she stated that the assassination was the freedmen's calamity, she wrote with an uncanny prescience. Emily Howland seemed to instinctively recognize that her people would ultimately bear the greatest loss as a consequence of Booth's action. Her life, since it was inexplicably bound to the lives of those freedmen in Virginia, would be touched by this calamity and the course she may have charted for herself and the freedmen was now to be drastically altered.

5

Journey to Arcadia

As spring moved into early summer, changes began to take place in the Virginia countryside. The muddy roads hardened and dried as the spring rains ended. The seeds planted in the fields and private gardens surrounding the freedmen's camps and villages were now blossoming forth promising an adequate harvest of essential crops. The passage of the Freedmen's Bureau Act on March 3, 1865 had also heralded a more promising future for the residents of these Virginia communities. With this Act the Bureau of Refugees, Freedmen and Abandoned Lands was established to aid and protect the newly acquired rights of blacks in the period of postwar adjustment. This agency was to be responsible for alleviating the physical deprivations of those Southern blacks and ensuring the reasonable reorganization of Southern agricultural lands.

Even after Lincoln's death hope ran high among those involved with the freedmen in the Virginia counties near the nation's capital. Teachers, missionaries and civilian officers all saw the fledgling government agency as capable of taking over the direction and care of the blacks. With sighs of relief they saw their present exhausting work drawing to a close. The fate of the blacks no longer rested in their hands but was to be guided by wiser political heads on the national level.

As Emily Howland made her circuit to the outlying villages around Falls Church that spring, her thoughts kept returning to her own home and family in Sherwood. Sallie Holley, Caroline Putnam and many other friends working in the camps and villages had already left their positions to journey to their homes for needed rest and relaxation. By mid-July Emily too decided to return home feeling tired and uncertain about her future and in need of the coolness and quiet beauty to be found in her rural New York community.

She did not journey alone however. A fifteen year old black girl named Susy Baker accompanied her on the three day trip to Sherwood and spent the rest of the summer by Emily's side. Emily had first met Susy in Georgetown and shortly thereafter made her a teaching assistant in one of the freedmen's schools on her Virginia circuit. Emily was now loathe to have Susy remain in Virginia or to return to the Baker home in Georgetown. Emily felt the summer living in Sherwood would be far more healthful and beneficial to Susy. Before their departure north in mid-July, Emily prepared her family for Susy's arrival and her sister-in-law Hannah with her usual gracious warmth and tact began to plan family picnics, rides and boat trips on the lake for Emily and Susy.

Such divertisements may have been soothing for Emily. With her arrival home she was guaranteed a respite from her physical labor, but with it came hours filled with reflection on both the future of her freedmen friends and her own uncertain status. She felt that she had satisfactorily resolved the issue of being a single woman and a social activist. Having examined the ramifications of this position years earlier, she had then moved into a field of endeavor that left little time for further introspection or analysis. Now she had time once again to examine the details of her personal as well as political life.

As fall approached, Emily pondered the options that were being developed for the blacks by Federal authorities and questioned her sense of obligation to those black families formerly under her care. Her sense of commitment to these families had not died. With her inherent distrust of institutionalized philanthropy and governmental agencies her concern for these families in fact grew as the strength and direction of the Freedmen's Bureau began to ebb and waver in the unsettled political atmosphere of Washington. Tired, and wanting to believe that the government was capable of taking over her job, she had left Virginia saying that her efforts were no longer needed since there would be "the good times coming" for her people with the advent of the Freedmen's Bureau Act. Now after a prolonged rest she was questioning the accuracy of her statement as new and more immediate obligations arose.

Her mother remained in poor condition and Emily had to finally face and acknowledge Hannah's long-held wish. She wanted Emily, her unmarried female child, to remain by her side during her final years. Aunt Rebecca ever concerned with the family's problems joined Hannah in reminding Emily of her familial duties. "Oh our children, our unmarried children, how our hearts cling to them in advanced life as they cheer and comfort many otherwise gloomy and monotonous moments confined at home with very little that is cheerful." Although other female relatives wrote similar expressions of concern and advice to Emily, Hannah Letchworth Howland refused to join in and pressure her sister-in-law in this fashion. This kind, sympathetic and reserved woman had quietly assumed the responsibility of caring for her mother-in-law shortly after her marriage to William and appeared to recognize and meet the diverse needs of the individuals in this family. Dating from the writing of their Whig petition in 1844 Hannah and Emily had shared a warm and loving friendship, finding in each other the sister they had never known in childhood. Emily automatically assumed that Hannah understood her needs and motivations more clearly than other members of her family, and she was never disappointed in this assumption. More than once Hannah had shouldered Emily's domestic and familial duties so that Emily might be able to put her energy and talent into activities outside the home.

Slocum had obviously accepted Emily's choice of an activist life style and her single status—choices which elicited mixed expressions of grudging enthusiasm and bemusement over his daughter's independence and concern for the freedmen. Slocum was more in accord with Emily's desire to put her humanistic ideals into practice than was her mother. At no time can a loving bond between mother and daughter be found in Emily's voluminous writings. They appear in fact to have been strangers to each other; their correspondence is characterized by a striking psychological and emotional distance. Unfortunately before her death Emily decided to edit or destroy certain information regarding her relationship with family and friends in her correspondence and journals. Significantly, she left behind little record of her mother. This absence stands in sharp contrast with the great wealth of information she offered about other family members.

More important, the sketchy portrait that Emily drew and preserved of her mother, although respectful, is decidedly unflattering; Hannah was severe, pious, unhappy, sickly, complaining, frugal and withdrawn. In the context of this portrait it is difficult to fully understand why Emily again succumbed to the pressure to care for her aging mother during the fall of 1865 and for the first time in four years remained at home. Her decision to stay with Hannah despite the pleas of her activist friends to return to Virginia points to the strength of the ties holding Emily to her Sherwood home.

Other things point to the intensity of this newest period of indecision for Howland. In articles written for the local newspapers and a national periodical she spoke as though the activist phase of her life's work had ended with the close of the war and Lincoln's death. She confidently informed Colonel John Eaton of the Freedmen's Bureau in the spring of 1865 that although "the school had become my life" she rejoiced "that the care of the freedmen during their transition state has at last fallen to those who are interested, who understand them and their wants."

But by late summer, Emily had already begun to write critically of the ignorance of the Freedmen's Bureau and their policy of non-support for the education of blacks. Physical relief for the freedmen was provided by the agency but their education was sponsored by ever-diminishing voluntary funds from private benevolent associations. She wrote with evident annoyance that "one of the first acts of our wise freedmen's bureau is to deprive teachers of their rations after the first of next mo. Poor policy for a free gov't, it should feed the teachers as long as these gov't camps remain." Another irksome problem Emily recognized was that many teachers and missionaries were losing their small salaries from freedmen's relief and missionary societies.

Although six hundred miles distant in Sherwood, Emily developed a firm grasp on the situation evolving between freedmen, teachers, Federal agency and the aid associations. She managed to secure teaching positions with small monthly incomes for both Anna Searing and Reverend Johnson in the vicinity of Freedmen's Village, while placing her cousins Sarah and Benjamin Alsop to work on a government farm in St. Mary's County, Maryland. Letters from either Searing, Holley, the Alsops or Johnson arrived at least weekly throughout November and December asking for Emily's assistance or advice in handling the often confusing, quickly deteriorating relations between freedmen and the Bureau. Her sympathy for the freedmen's situation had always been evident. She had written earlier that year of the troubles developing between the government and freedmen. "The lines are being drawn tighter all the time, no women are allowed to work in the field now. This is grievous to some. Poor things they are to see hard times yet before their status is settled and I think the nation will too." Frequent government regulations appeared that seemed to Emily insensitive to the needs of the freedmen and unnecessarily restrictive for those within government's camps and villages. Efforts were made by the Bureau to force the blacks to sign contracts by the first of the new year to work for the white overseers of abandoned plantations. On the other hand many freedmen were reluctant to sign for they had heard rumors of the "mule and forty acres."

By January appeals to Emily had become strident. No one among her friends could understand her staying in Sherwood in light of her knowledge and criticism of the situation in Virginia; but in this case, she was capable of withstanding the pressure of her friends more easily than the pressure of her family. Officials from the Philadelphia Freedmen's Relief Association, government agents and the New York Missionary Association all wrote requesting her to return to the settlements around Freedmen's Village to coordinate the efforts of missionaries, teachers and government workers. As in the contraband camps during the war, there was no bureaucratic structure existing in which she could find a vacant position into which she could step. If she were to return to Virginia, it would be to work in a non-official capacity as she had done earlier. It appeared that someone was needed to bring about a semblance of order and to open communications between and among blacks, teachers, government officials and missionaries. Emily however steadfastly continued to hold her own counsel in trying to determine her own capability to take on this new responsibility. She refused to reveal her future plans as the contradictory demands of family and then freedmen were presented to her.

Emily and Slocum discussed the freedmen's predicament frequently during the long winter. Starting a project she had long deferred Emily began to paint her father's portrait after the first of the year. During the long sessions their conversations dwelt in part on the subject most often in Emily's thoughts—her future. A talented artist, Emily could easily have become absorbed in painting and drawing and on more than one occasion that winter wistfully looked to the day when painting would be the primary activity in her life.

But by March the portrait was finished and their idyll had ended. Sometime in March Emily decided to return South. Reiterating a key theme that she nevertheless would deny at different points in her life, she said that she must again subscribe to "a cheerful love of doing all one is capable of, hence fulfilling one's mission." Slocum understood his daughter's motivations in setting off with Susy Baker for Washington on April 3. In their discussions, Emily had predicted the failure of Bureau and associations to cope with the needs of freedmen in the years to come. That winter Emily had formulated an alternative plan to smooth the difficult transition for certain black families from freedom status to full citizenship. The abandoned lands of former slavemasters in Virginia were being sold by the government to interested parties at ridiculously low prices. Slocum had pledged to Emily sufficient funds to purchase a few hundred acres of prime farm land and acquiesced in her wish that she control all aspects of the venture. The Alsops were requested to look for such land for sale in their Maryland county while Emily, now in Washington, scouted the Virginia territory.

Emily's enthusiasm was at a high pitch, very much in tune with the bustling activity in the Capital that spring. She returned Susy to her family in Georgetown and quickly sought out her close friends Emma Brown and Anna Searing and together they visited government agencies that could assist in Emily's plan. After examining information that officials had given her she next visited with the Bowens and Johnsons. With their help she studied the feasibility of assuming a supervisory role as suggested earlier by freedmen's associations and her friends. Emily frequently mentioned to her father that she should receive a small salary for her work from the Philadelphia Friends Freedmen's Relief Association and from the New York Missionary Association as a matter of principle and not out of need. If they did pay her during the years 1866–1868, no record can be found of it in either the associations' or her private accounts. Slocum continued to support her, giving her money for all her needs whenever requested.

Growing increasingly dissatisfied with the relative inactivity while waiting to put her plan into motion, Emily decided that she could handle the supervisory job of coordinating freedmen's education in the Freedmen's Village area. Although not paid by the Freedmen's Bureau and not listed in their records, she nevertheless must have received at least the Bureau's tacit approval to live and work in camps under their control. If freedmen's aid associations did not pay her, they did support the teachers under her supervision. She was working in a highly unstructured situation once again where smooth organizational functioning was non-existent. When a new educational need or problem arose she found herself searching for new methods to utilize the meager resources of interested associations or the Bureau to overcome the problem.

Since educational efforts made by associations and the Bureau appeared to be uncoordinated and at times overlapping, Emily decided to canvass her district to determine how extensive the needs and problems were. Within a week she was walking five miles a day and riding thirteen miles on the back of a broken-down cart pulled by a feeble horse to district schools. Her letters to her superiors pointed to the shocking lack of order and coordination among those parties involved solely with freedmen's education. The Freedmen's Bureau was responsible for supplying school facilities, the associations for supplies and subsistence salaries for the teachers and missionary societies for personnel and their boarding facilities. Schools were held in dilapidated rooms, dimly lit, overcrowded and understaffed. Supplies were inadequate and in some cases non-existent while the sessions were held on a sporadic basis with no consistent educational goals in view. Seeing the need was the worst at Hall's Hill, Emily prepared to make a nearby vacant cottage her base camp but not without reservations about the loneliness that could arise by living in this isolated spot alone. She questioned how she would be able to endure existence here, but this concern was short-lived since her schedule rarely permitted her leisure time.

In addition to teaching at Hall's Hill she visited the other schools under her responsibility and each evening walked to Fort Ethan Allen to teach in the school for black soldiers that she had helped establish with a Mrs. Wilson. Although wearied by this pace, Emily acted as spokeswoman and arbiter in matters between blacks and the Bureau. Her relaxation from duty consisted of visiting with Susy and with those black families who were now her friends as well as neighbors. She had known some of these families since contraband camp days and felt a deep concern for their future. Her journal is full of warm and sympathetic sketches of Aunt Charity; Lucy, Sarah and Uncle Moses; Cain and Benjamin. Uncle Moses was most frequently mentioned and it appears that with him she had established a close relationship, best depicted in this story from her journal. Moses visited her one day rather upset and feeling anxious. Finally he told Howland that her Quakerism, or more specifically her lack of baptism by water, was the source of his concern. She told him that "he must enlarge his faith and make it broad enough to take me in without baptism," but "he could not see how" saying "I wants to meet you up dar. I don't want you to be lost." Howland was touched that "the one they loved, they thought must go to everlasting woe."

Emily spoke with compassion for the elderly Aunt Charity whose failing sight and hearing made life difficult during these years. More than once, she took additional supplies to her to alleviate her suffering in her final years. Her tone when discussing Charity was one of respect. She listened to Charity's and Moses' stories of their lives and recorded them in her journal along with other freedmen's biographies. She would frequently lapse into idiomatic speech when recording, but in this instance, Emily was not exercising a sense of superiority or paternalism. Their cares had obviously become one of Emily's primary concerns. As a result of these warm relationships educational and economic goals governing her project slowly came into existence.

Emily had first intervened on behalf of the freedmen in a government matter the previous spring when abuse of a number of freedmen's children by a civilian employer was brought to her attention by a military officer who was reluctant to become involved. She went directly to Captain Brown the military official in charge of the Mason Island camp with the problem. She requested that the Captain assume responsibility in this case and insisted that the children be returned to proper care. This action endeared her more to the blacks than to the Federal officers and the Bureau. Her name became familiar to the Assistant Commissioner of the Bureau when she returned to Virginia in 1866 and became embroiled in several incidents with racial overtones.

In April she appeased the white male military community when animosity developed after white soldiers had been insulted by black soldiers and children in her Camp Rucker school. Four months later she chastized the assistant commissioner and local superintendent for their neglect of certain freedmen near Freedmen's Village. She next made public the complaints of black soldiers of the 101st USCT regarding alleged mishandling of their funds by the white manager of the Freedmen's Savings and Banking Institute. By the end of 1866 she had smoothly showed another aspect of her personality, that of mediator when sensitive issues arose between freedmen and their white caretakers.

She had assumed that many of the black families would follow the Bureau's prodding and return to start their lives anew in those counties where they had been slaves, but most were either too poor or too sick to travel. The younger healthier men had left Freedmen's Village during the winter in time to begin spring planting on five or ten acres of their old plantation, leaving their families behind to eke out a living on government or unclaimed land around the forts and villages. White speculators could also be found in these Virginia tidewater counties as they traveled in search of prime agricultural land at a cheap price. One such speculator was Edward Nash, a lower-middle class former civil servant and part-time politician from Washington. Emily had made the Nashs' acquaintance in Washington years earlier at the Miner School and renewed it in 1866 at Fort Morton. Arriving at Fort Morton with his wife and children, Nash followed a number of freedmen to Northumberland County in hope of finding land, work and possibly a few extra dollars to feed his ever-growing family. Showing a lack of good judgment Emily had included Nash in her new venture, commissioning him to find suitable land for her to purchase. Nash had managed to gain the trust and respect of some black families in Freedmen's Village and he obviously informed them of Howland's project. Within days, Emily was approached by so many black families asking to live on her prospective land that she laughingly wrote Hannah that before long she would have to drive them away from her door.

Emily now began to advocate the importance of a policy of self-help among blacks and the need to develop local black leadership In a number of small ways she strove to act upon her own advice, although every gain in black autonomy meant a reduction of the power and superiority that was a basis for her own fragile autonomy. Such actions show how strong and determined Emily had grown in her advocacy of human equality. Although she had been instructed by the Bureau to parcel out enough seeds to sustain one hundred families around her settlement, she had them distributed by a black preacher whom the families knew and respected. She began working on schemes whereby more blacks, such as the preacher, would be placed in positions of authority. Within weeks she had included the black community's unofficial leaders in the collection and distribution of the village's allotment of food and clothing. Emily felt that their lack of knowledge of the fundamentals of economy and a monetary system was due to "their training in slavery, suspicious & unimpressible as a stone wall," but then qualified the statement by adding that "the people among whom I have lived for the past two years are a very much higher order of beings." The negative categories in which she placed freedmen as a group were never applicable to those few whom she knew intimately. She proudly related to her father that *her* black friends went through the winter without once visiting the "drawing house" and received charity only when voluntarily made. That they could possess such economy and "real elevation of the mind" convinced Emily that their fellow blacks could also make this transition successfully.

She felt the key to such a transition rested in the adoption of a teaching plan previously unused in her district. Taking into account that the entire family probably needed educational training, she worked on the assumption that her day pupils were learning not only for themselves but for their parents. The type of knowledge therefore needed immediately by adults as well as children to successfully cope with economic complexities of post-war life would be given the highest priority. Arithmetic figures were taught first for obvious reasons. She next gave her attention to instructing pupils to read and write script since letters were a necessity if families scattered by war and numerous government relocations were to be reunited.

Once these rudimentary skills were mastered, progress toward the ultimate goal could be made. Emily wanted the freedmen to "become a sober, industrious, law abiding people as capable of using the elective franchise for their own and their country's interest as the majority of the people who now possess that right."

Under the Freedmen's Bureau, she felt that such progress could not be made. As she told her sister-in-law Hannah, it had reached the point where she felt she must keep her eyes shut to the brutal, dehumanizing conditions in which the freedmen lived if she were to function properly. It was painful for her to think of thousands of people around her half famished due to overwork and underfeeding. Only by constant begging on her part could Emily obtain enough supplies to keep the old, infirmed and orphans from greater deprivation. In addition to these problems, the summer was unseasonably cold and she found herself dreading the coming of winter, not seeing where enough food could be found to cook and to warm the freedmen's shanties.

Emily felt she could postpone her project no longer. She began to think in more concrete terms about her plan. She would purchase a tract of land in a racially mixed rural Virginia community and place a small number of her freedmen friends on the land. Although retaining ownership of the land at first, she would let the families buy it from her as the venture became more financially stable. Adopting the standard white upper and middle class attitude toward poverty at this time, she advocated a policy of self-help, feeling it unwise to give her friends the land as a gift.

Regardless of her confidence in the freedmen Emily continued to question their ability to cope with economic realities to be encountered on the farm. She had no doubt that they understood the mechanics of farming far better than she, but she lacked faith in their ability to market their products, plan for the next year and avoid the credit squeeze. Her condescending attitude toward her freedmen friends arose quite naturally out of the basically unequal relationship between Emily as the economic superior and the blacks as her dependents.

Emily also wished to protect her friends from that emerging class of white Northerners and Southerners who were taking economic and political advantage of their more ignorant black brothers. Finally she reasoned that the blacks would appreciate and use their land to better advantage if they had to work for it. Pulling oneself up by the bootstrap was a philosophy truly highly valued.

Not to be overlooked is the fact that by retaining ownership she could continue to exert her influence on the project. Owning and managing a black farming community would require her presence in Northumberland and provide her with a socially approved role as a humanitarian-philanthropist—a role that was a welcome option since she at times continued to feel stigmatized for rejecting the more traditional, if limited, roles open to her as a single woman.

Emily divulged specific details of her plan first to her father. Since early spring Nash had been eyeing two tracts of land in Northumberland County on a fourteen mile wide peninsula between the Potomac and Rappahannock Rivers. Uncle Moses Washington and Lewis Carter had formerly been slaves in that county and were familiar with the quality of land, farming procedures and crops. Emily was amused to see role reversal take place when they began to instruct her on the modes of managing Virginia farmland. She was nevertheless impressed with their knowledge and suggested that she might enter such an enterprise if they could help her make it economically successful.

Emily's letters to her mother however dealt with a different aspect of the project. She realized that Hannah would view this venture primarily in terms of the lengthy separations and infrequent communication it would entail. She attempted to explain the reasons motivating her at that time. "I think a good deal about that plan. It always seems to me what I ought to do. It would be a permanent benefit where one's purpose could be carried to something like completeness. In my present course, it is a little in one place and then another."

Anxious to get the project underway, Emily traveled to Northumberland the first week of June to inspect two tracts of land under consideration. She dispassionately examined all aspects of the situation from the soil, means of fertilization, crop abundance, wood supply and water power, to the attitude of neighbors toward Northerners and blacks, the need for schools, and the current bargaining price of land in the area. In a glowing report to Slocum, Emily found little to discourage her. Although the few white inhabitants of the area were understandably bitter over the loss of their labor and extensive land holdings, they were all cordial to her. She spoke with members of the black population about construction of a school near Heathsville, the county seat, and was encouraged to find this met with eager approval.

Optimistic that she had found a suitable place, Emily authorized Nash to examine the records and title and to proceed with the purchase. Nash had recently become the owner of a neighboring tract and had found, as was generally the case in Virginia in 1866, that the landowner was in great need of money. Bargaining began in earnest and Emily exhibited a financial shrewdness that rivaled her father's well-known ability to gain from another's economic misfortune. Although the asking price was $10 per acre, by the close of the summer she succeeded in paying approximately $5 per acre for a 317 acre tract near Heathsville. When the purchase was finalized the hitherto pragmatic Emily romantically christened her experiment Arcadia. The Romans and, later, European poets characterized the ancient Arcadian shepherds and farmers as the ideal of innocence and virtue. Emily, in thus naming her project, continued this romantic tradition and revealed those qualities for which she hoped the new Arcadians would be known—simplicity, piety, hospitality, honesty and kindness. This was truly going to be the promised land for those few fortunate enough to accompany her.

Dissatisfaction arose only when Emily began to make the final arrangements among the freedmen. Three extended families were to be the first colonists in Arcadia, although in old age Emily wrote that she took four families. She had refused to have more people accompany her for she felt that her project would fail if she heavily populated the acreage at such an early date. To leave so many behind in the poverty of Freedman's Village caused her much unhappiness, but she hoped that in Arcadia she would be setting an example. She looked forward to the day when other Arcadias would dot the Virginia countryside, filled with hard-working freedmen from the Village.

Deteriorating conditions within the camp added to her uneasiness. The Philadelphia Friends Freedmen's Association refused her latest requests for materials and aid for blacks at Falls Church since they could barely support their teachers elsewhere in the South. Shortly thereafter the Pennsylvania Freedman's Relief Association notified her that after the first of the year all operations in the Virginia area were to be halted. Voluntary funds that had flowed into the coffers of freedmen's aid associations during the war had slowed down to a trickle throughout the year of 1866, leaving the Washington-Virginia area hardest hit. The government planned to stop all rations on the first of October, leaving freedmen in a state bordering on total disorder. This was one response of the Freedmen's Bureau to the two-pronged criticism by Northern philanthropists and Southern landowners that food and clothing rations were in part responsible for keeping healthy black men and women idle and unemployed at a time when their labor was needed to work land through-out the South.

From this unpleasant scene the first black families "set sail for the promised land" in the cold, dreary first week of December. Uncle Moses Washington, Lewis Carter and Benjamin Tolliver headed the families that traveled by the Steamboat *Columbia* to Arcadia that week. Uncle Moses was the unofficial partriarch of the colony, leading the families with a sense of dignity, warmth, com-mon sense, sternness and industry. Success or failure of the colony depended upon Uncle Moses, and the mutual respect and trust that had always existed between Moses and Emily augured a satisfactory first year. Although the winter was difficult they managed to build temporary homes and animal shelters, clear land for spring planting and sell wood for the necessary food purchases. Emily went to Arcadia for a one week visit in December but did not return there again until May. She did not stay to see the project through; instead she once more turned her back to the freedmen and headed to her Sherwood home. But she left her colony confident that in Uncle Moses' hands the small group would survive the winter well.

As Arcadia moved smoothly off the drawing board and onto the soil of Northumberland County, Emily was not able to enjoy the inner quiet and satisfaction that generally accompanies a successful venture. By the end of 1866, Emily had been forced to deal with a number of new, unexpected emotions. After a month long illness Susy Baker, Emily's young black teaching assistant, friend and close companion since contraband camp days died in the final days of September, 1866. Emily had spent much of September with Susy, first at the Freedmen's Village and later in Washington. She tried to prepare the sixteen year old girl for death, nursing her, giving her comfort and emotional support and helping her resign her spirit to the inevitable. Emily was twenty-four years older than Susy and in caring for her, maternal feelings either long overlooked or suppressed came to the fore.

Years earlier Emily had taken Susy under wing, bringing her along to Sherwood, Philadelphia and from camp to camp during and after the war. She had educated Susy and had recently secured a permanent teaching position for her with the freedmen. Emily quite probably had planned to complete her education at Oberlin College as in the early 1860s she had similarly helped her first black female friend, Emma Brown.

Other single women during this period raised young girls, bringing them to work, live and be educated in their homes. Dr. Elizabeth Blackwell's legal adoption of a young girl was a notable example, while Myrtilla Miner's unofficial adoption of the responsibility of raising a number of female children followed the more popular course. In this context, Emily's relationship with Susy was not unusual. What was extraordinary was the transracial aspect of their association and Emily's reaction to their relationship.

Emily and Susy spent the night before Susy's death alone sharing a warm companionship and reliving their many experiences together over the past few years. Emily had returned to Freedmen's Village the day Susy died, but went immediately back to the city to mourn with the Baker family. In describing Susy's final hours to Hannah Emily wrote in terms similar to those that a mother would use when her child had died. Quite incidentally, Emily in this same letter revealed the natural animosity that could arise between a biological and a surrogate mother and in doing so reassured herself that she had the larger part of Susy's love. "I think she (Mrs. Baker) never felt satisfied that she had the second place in Susy's affections. Once in the night the poor child looking at me said, 'O Miss Howland I love you so much . . .'"

If at all possible, Emily in her grief would have turned to Emma Brown and Anna Searing for comfort and understanding. Unfortunately for Emily Anna Searing had felt her services could best be rendered teaching in a Bureau project in Farmville, Virginia and by mid-September had already left Washington. Meanwhile Emma Brown had been facing severe crises arising from several deaths among family and friends that summer and fall, and the loss of her teaching position. If Emma and Anna had not been thus preoccupied their response to Emily's suffering may have been far different. When Emily sought Emma she found herself giving Emma comfort and strength as the wiser, older friend. Similarly in her correspondence with Anna, Emily responded by giving maternal advice about Anna's duties with the freedmen rather than expressing her grief. Emma and Anna continued to view Emily as undaunted and invincible in the face of such personal adversity. Thus it was only to Hannah Letchworth Howland that Emily could unburden her sorrow and their correspondence during this period attests to the unique and important role Hannah continued to play in Emily's life as sister, friend and comforter.

For the past decade Emily had remained friends with the Danas and the Bowens, two families who had helped her through the upsetting final days at Miner's school. Both families respected Emily and her work in Washington and Virginia. Emily in turn was thankful for their wise counsel and assistance in matters both personal and public. They had provided her with a warm home to visit when in Washington, friendship and intelligent conversation. Their awareness of changing political and military situations had helped her in her work on more than one occasion.

Now after Susy's death and as the winter approached Emily found herself spending an increasing amount of time in their company. Mr. Dana had become a major-general and was unofficially attached to the Freedmen's Bureau under the supervision of his friend General Oliver O. Howard. In the close military community in Georgetown Dana had made the acquaintance of an intelligent, witty and compassionate Bostonian named Charles W. Folsom. Folsom had recently been promoted to the rank of colonel and was attached to the Quartermaster General's Office in Washington that fall. He began to spend many of his non-duty hours in the company of the Danas, as did Emily. Presumably he met her for the first time in the Danas' Georgetown home. Both Folsom and Emily were intelligent, independent, unmarried and approaching forty, and the Danas most likely encouraged their growing friendship. Day trips to Point Lookout on the Chesapeake Bay and weekend visits to friends' country homes included Emily and Folsom. Emily, who for four years had rarely mentioned her wearing apparel, began to write home for velvet bonnets and frilly aprons. That fall in her correspondence she defensively characterized herself as an actor, not a narrator, who was too involved in her activities to be able to catch the romance in the reality of her life. These incidents may well represent Emily's response to the continued attentions of Colonel Folsom. When she made her December visit to Northumberland Emily significantly omitted in writing to her father that Colonel Folsom had accompanied her to Arcadia to survey the land and prepare a map for her. Emily, who had previously kept her own counsel in matters pertaining to her beloved project, was now sharing her plans and aspirations with the Colonel.

Folsom and Emily shared a major common interest in the welfare of the blacks. They agreed that only through education could black women and men live successfully in economic independence with full civil rights. Folsom agreed with Emily's Arcadia, feeling it an acceptable alternative to the inefficient and faltering plans of the Bureau in the Northumberland District. After the December trip to Arcadia Folsom began to help the colony in earnest. When Emily arrived home in Sherwood at the end of December a letter was waiting for her from the Colonel. She had requested from the Bureau eight sashes being stored in Freedmen's Village, for use in erecting a school near her land in Northumberland. Folsom had received a copy of her letter from a friend at the Bureau and not only sent them on the Steamer *Columbia* to Heathsville but also had included sixteen new windows and a grindstone. Emily, who had given so much to others, was now beginning to receive, since ten of those windows were to be for a house of her own. To ease the discomfort he knew she would feel Folsom laughingly wrote that it "was little enough to do & there is no danger of my going to heaven too easily by hanging my benevolence in this way on lines that other people have stretched."

Emily obviously must have confided in Folsom her plans to live on a more permanent basis in Heathsville—plans which she had not shared with her parents. She may have been returning to Sherwood in part to seek her parents understanding and approval of her plans for living in Heathsville. But as her mother's physical condition steadily worsened over the winter, Emily was forced to postpone her return trip to Virginia and willingly assumed the responsibility of caring for her mother.

Word of her project had begun to spread and Emily soon found Arcadia being helped by unexpected sources. The Bureau decided that her proposed school house would be an excellent site for a Bureau-sponsored school and helped with construction and supplies. Next the Friends Freedmen Association in Philadelphia once again appointed her as a teacher to labor among her friends. Finally, old abolitionist and contraband camp friends began to volunteer their services in the Northumberland District. Emily, who had conceived Arcadia as an alternative to federal policy, was now finding education of the people of Arcadia creeping under government control.

By the end of April she could wait in Sherwood no longer while Arcadia slipped away from her. She allowed the school building to be placed under jurisdiction of the Assistant Commissioner of the

Bureau of Refugees, Freedmen and Abandoned Lands' Virginia Department, but insisted on having free rein in all educational matters.

With her daily presence on the farm, Emily felt she could effectively counteract detrimental actions or policies on the part of the Bureau's Northumberland District agent. She hoped that her freedmen farmers would set a worthy example for other Heathsville freedmen to follow. Attending school and church, learning to read, write and transact business, to realize the responsibility of voting and self-government and to successfully manage their farms were goals she expected each member of the three Arcadia families to ultimately achieve.

Within a month she felt confident that the Bureau, the freedmen and she could coexist peacefully in the Northumberland region and wrote to her friends of the pressing need for dedicated teachers with experience in dealing with both freedmen and the Bureau. Sallie Holley and Carrie Putnam, Emily's old friends from the Philadelphia group fit this description well. Their lives during the sixties reflected their concern with the fate of black Americans. Like Emily, they had raised funds for and worked in the freedmen's relief camps in the South and written numerous articles for Northern journals on the plight of freedmen. Considered strong-minded, active women, they were now casting about the dismal Freedmen's Village in Virginia trying unsuccessfully to alleviate poverty among the remaining villagers. They heard Emily's call for help and joyfully traveled to Heathsville to begin again in a more auspicious environment.

As in abolition days Holley was the more dominant and better-known of this unusual twosome while Caroline Putnam remained the quiet, industrious worker who put Holley's ideas into practice. These two women had continued to function smoothly as a unit and until 1867 seemed inseparable. Significantly, they always spoke of themselves in the first person plural. Their devotion to each other was rivaled only by their dedication to the freedmen. When they joined Emily in Virginia, Sallie Holley set about establishing the Holley School in neighboring Lottsburgh. While she organized necessary support, teachers and equipment, Carrie Putnam quietly began to meet people and to teach in a makeshift school in Lottsburgh. From this date on, Lottsburgh was Holley's and Putnam's home until their deaths. While Sallie continued to travel extensively for health and to find support for their school, Carrie remained at their home effectively running both school house and the post office over the next fifty years.

It is not difficult to image Emily, her youth behind her, settling in neighboring Heathsville. Emily hinted that at one time she had hoped for a quiet, satisfying, full life in Northumberland similar to that of her neighbor and friend from the Philadelphia group, Caroline Putnam.

When she arrived in Heathsville in April, Emily boarded with the Nashes while deciding on the type of house to build for herself. She supervised the construction of desks and benches for the school by black carpenters hired by the District's agent. Next she canvassed the immediate district to determine the number of students, black and white, who would be attending the primary grades. In meeting her neighbors, she realized that there were rigid social distinctions in the community between wealthy landowners, poor whites and blacks with "the castes very strongly marked." Her first duty was to assure members of all three groups that their children were welcome at her school. She guessed quite correctly that landowners would prefer to send their children to the white school in Heathsville, but did expect to see poor whites and blacks join together for education at her school house. She felt that the poor whites and blacks "both now regard the Yankees as their friends."

The black students began to fill the school daily in early May with an average attendance of thirty. She felt that this was "the ideal school I had never hoped to find where the young minds were ready to be led without pinching, jostling or tricks. It seems to me that I must hitherto have taught a reform school." Theodore Dow a Northerner and neighbor helped as an assistant and together they began a night school at the request of black adults in the vicinity. It was at this point that she realized that even more schools and teachers were needed in the district and urged aid associations to provide more stipends for additional teachers.

Uncle Aleck one of the few black freedmen fortunate enough to buy land in the area was recognized as a leader by both residents of Arcadia and the surrounding black community. Aleck and Emily had discussed the need for a new building to be erected on her land for use as a church and school. At the end of May, Aleck and Emily marked the ground and construction was soon progressing at a good pace. With an unusual blending of sardonic humor, confidence and a sense of superiority, she told her father that the freedmen intended to call her building "Howland Chapel." She preferred that if it must be named after her, it would at least be called the Howland School for "a school is what I would like my name perpetuated by. Preaching is darkness or no light when practiced by ignorance and conceit. I never saw such a perfect mixture of both as the minister of these people. It pains me that they can have nothing better. I hope I may help them to outgrow him." And the erection of the Howland School was to be the first step in this growth process.

Although teaching and her farm occupied many of her hours, she was not as unaware of the activities of the Heathsville community as she at times feigned. In her letters home she delighted in relating stories which circulated about her within the black and white communities. "While quietly pursuing my busy way the echos of gossip which reach my ears, intimate I am the exciting topic in this region, a person about whom there are decided and antagonistic opinions, probably the best abused & best praised woman in the county."

There is no doubt that the "school teacher" or "nigger teacher," depending upon the point of view of the speaker, roused the curiosity of land owners, poor whites and blacks alike. Whenever away from the farm Emily dressed in her finest clothes, hoping to perpetuate the existing impression that she was a grand city lady; she justified this un-Quakerly attitude by saying such actions lent the cause prestige. Although admitting that she was always courteously treated, Emily harbored the thought that the Southern landowners were decidely antagonistic toward her and were saying "their spiteful things out of my hearing and very spiteful they are."

Herein lies one of those paradoxes in Emily's personality that emerges from time to time. Emily, who exhibited so much compassion and tolerance for those in a less fortunate position, refused to view white landowning Southerners with anything but a deep-seated contempt. Years of absorbing spurious as well as serious abolitionist literature had conditioned her to classify white inhabitants of the former slave states as uncivilized people lacking a sense of justice and an understanding of the world beyond the plantation. Finally, she held them directly responsible for the degradation of the blacks and for the bloodiest war in United States history; she could not forgive them on either count.

When visiting Harper's Ferry in July on a pilgrimage with Sallie, Carrie and other friends from the Philadelphia group, Emily was impressed with the Southerners she met since they confirmed her opinion of them. "They, none of them, know what they think, are clearly united on two points, hatred of Yankees & admiration of rebel generals." Even when overt hostility toward her did not materialize, Emily continued to think the worst of her white upper class neighbors, refused to accept their civility and projected her negative opinions upon them. To no class or group did she so thoroughly close her mind, remaining blind and intractable on this point until her death.

Her faith in her poor white neighbors was rewarded only a month after the opening of school, for the first white student entered the freedmen's schoolhouse, causing quite a stir in the district. She acknowledged that it took no little heroism on the part of both the child and the parents and viewed it as the first hopeful event in the poor white family in generations. She thought that the school eventually would become public, and therefore made a special effort to encourage the children of both races to attend. It was the adult night school however that most quickly fulfilled Emily's hopes; within weeks more than forty men and women, black and white, faithfully attended her classes. After working all day, many walked as far as five and six miles to receive an hour's instruction from her.

Their enthusiasm to learn gave her deep satisfaction but also made her redouble her efforts to find salaries, supplies, schoolhouses and teachers for the Sixth Bureau District. New York Freedmen's Association had closed their doors to her as the American Missionary Association had done earlier. The Pennsylvania Freedmen's Relief Association offered a number of limited salaries; Philadelphia Friends Freedmen Association offered books and supplies and the Bureau provided transportation for the teachers. White and black residents in the county opened their homes, providing free room and board in most cases to the teachers. Sallie Holley began lecturing to raise funds for both the Lottsburgh and Heathsville schools and placed letters in the *Anti-Slavery Standard* to catch the sympathetic eye of a wealthy philanthropist.

Slocum conferred a larger income on Emily which she gratefully accepted. This first year in Arcadia was quickly draining the financial reserves she had managed to save from her allowance and her

Virginia job. Seed had to be bought and instruments purchased to plant, weed and harvest the oat, clover, corn and sweet potato crop. Cows, pigs and mules were necessities, and barns and fences needed to be built by the end of summer. Finally, food and cloth had to be purchased by Emily until the crops were harvested and sold.

When her teaching ended each afternoon, Emily would turn her attention to managing the farm. Most decisions were made with Uncle Moses although Emily occasionally consulted her father about major purchases. As in contraband and freedman camp days, she continued to teach the black women certain domestic skills of which they had no knowledge, most having been field hands when slaves. Cutting and sewing shirts and dresses, mending old clothes and shoes, preserving fruit and vegetables and baking were a few of the tasks she taught them in the late afternoon before supper and her night school began.

For the first time in her life the day's activities began to slip into a routine that pleased her. She wrote to her niece that "if it were not for the wood ticks, I should find nothing disagreeable here." Colonel Folsom had purchased a gentle roan for her to ride, knowing that this was one of the few recreations in which she indulged. The frequent showers made the roads muddy and walking difficult. She confessed to her niece that envying their freedom, she had started to imitate the children by making the trip to and from school barefoot, putting on shoes and stockings before she entered the schoolhouse door. As the temperature rose in July and the summer heat lasted late into the night, she took to sleeping under a large tree in the yard. A freedom and relaxation never felt in her youth was hers to enjoy during her fortieth summer.

As usual, to sister-in-law Hannah Emily divulged the political as well as the intimate details of her Northumberland life. In a particularly vivid letter, she described the political events taking place within the county leading up to the fall elections. Responsibility for the establishment of Reconstruction policy had passed from Andrew Johnson's hands into those of the Radical Republicans in Congress when the 1866 election brought Republicans and anti-Johnson majorities to both houses of Congress. With the First Reconstruction Act in March, 1867, the South had been divided into five military districts with Virginia becoming Military District Number One under General John M. Schofield. In successive acts the Southern states found it necessary for readmission to the Union to ratify the Fourteenth Amendment and to adopt state constitutions which provided for black suffrage. Emily saw the political rallies she described to Hannah as part of a campaign by three elements in Virginia attempting to become elected to the state constitutional convention to be held in Richmond in December, 1867. In this first step under Radical Reconstruction, scalawags (white Southerners who supported this policy of Radical Reconstruction), carpetbaggers (Northern political and economic opportunists) and blacks stumped across the state prior to the fall election and, to no one's surprise, found themselves in Richmond at the end of the year. The heavy hand of the Freedmen's Bureau was to be found at Heathsville meetings as well as in other Bureau Districts throughout the South. The Bureau's leading Heathsville officer, an unnamed lieutenant, had wisely ordered that no whiskey be sold at these political meetings so that the occasions would be as quiet and orderly as possible. These summer meetings also marked the beginning of the civilian Bureau agent's attempts to organize blacks in his district into the Republican party. Emily felt that local Bureau Agent Wilcox generally aligned with the Virginia Radical Republicans in "waving a bloody shirt." Composed of scalawags, carpetbaggers and after the passage of the Fifteenth Amendment the blacks, these Radical Republicans attempted to keep alive the issues of conflict and to identify the Democratic Party with the Confederacy and treason.

Emily, never capable of taking the role of the disinterested bystander, threw herself into the political activities wholeheartedly. She attended public meetings held by speakers of the Radical Republican Party and found herself once again acting as mediator between two conflicting forces. Events she described taking place in Heathsville on the fifth of July were repeated in small towns throughout Virginia that summer. "A thousand people men, women & children patiently, nay eagerly, standing to listen in the boiling July sun, from early morning until 6 P.M., after walking, some of them 20 miles, was a sight to inspire hope and confidence. Immediately around the speakers' stand were the jubilant emancipated, beyond them all about a fringe of chivalry, returned confederate soldiers, old planters, etc—quiet, grim & sad contrasting with the beaming glad faces of their former victims." Emily felt that by reason of Arcadia, her association with the Bureau and her antipathy toward that "fringe of chivalry," she would be perceived by all as aligned with the Radical Republicans. Instead she found that "my place seemed to be the medium between"; her sense of fairness overrode personal and political feelings and she cautiously agreed to step into this role. When a radical speaker, a former Union soldier, entered into a "splendid clashing of views with the youngsters of the vanquished cause" Emily admired the "out and out pluck" of both sides and encouraged them to be heard. When the same radical speaker came to Arcadia to organize the black men into a "loyal league" he insisted on calling it the Howland Loyal League. Emily voiced dissatisfaction with this league, feeling that such registration of loyal men in the district was "a rather disagreeable business." She was equally chagrined that they would name "something for me to which it denies admittance for women." In her attempts to be more moderate she now entertained doubts about the wisdom of those Northern whites in the county who were now taking a decidedly Radical Republican position.

The young radical speaker Dudley had not favorably impressed Emily with his enthusiasm to organize a loyalty league, but the effect she had upon him was far different. Within a week he had written to both General O. O. Howard and to General Orlando Brown about Emily Howland, Arcadia and the Bureau's school. In glowing terms he related that the work in Heathsville was progressing very favorably under Emily's auspices and that "she had accomplished one thing that so far is without precedent viz, she has induced several poor white children to enter her school and study and recite side by side with the colored children. She has an evening school for grown people, and so eager are they to learn that they fill her little room full each evening."

Critical of the inadequacy of the Bureau's schoolhouse, Dudley described construction underway at the Howland School and the urgent need for $200 worth of equipment to complete the project. Bureau inspectors were soon visiting Heathsville to assess the situation for themselves and returned to Richmond acknowledging that their funds would be wisely invested in the Howland School.

Although she wanted to complete construction on her school, Emily was hesitant to accept anything more from the Bureau and freedmen's aid associations. She felt strongly that if substantial financial help was given, it would place her in a disadvantageous position where she no longer would be sole leader of the educational aspect of her venture. She stressed to all involved in helping the Howland School that she "would not be compromised in any way—that if anything was best owed it must be *freely given*" so that she might "act with perfect freedom & without obligation to any sect or party."

Her impatience mounted as construction came to a halt, but she continued to stress this need for independence from the Bureau and relief associations. The school was finally finished that fall and if the Bureau did supply the necessary $200, no record exists of the transaction. The Howland School remained free of sectarian, military and political control until its incorporation into the Virginia public school system in the twentieth century.

Emily had been boarding with the Nashes while waiting for her house to be built on the land adjoining the Howland School. The Nashes were one of several families who opened their homes to fellow Northerners that summer when an influx of visitors descended upon this quiet backwater county. Colonel Folsom, James Ferree, Mary Reed and Cornelia Hancock were among the numbers who provided Howland with a few pleasant hours away from her teaching and farming responsibilities. In July when a band of teachers supported by the American Missionary Association arrived Emily was immediately drawn to a warm, kindly, wealthy, independent older woman in their midst, Laura Stebbins. Stebbins had raised and educated Theodore Dow, Emily's neighbor and assistant in the night school, and was responsible for the purchase of land Dow was now working. She was using this opportunity with the Association to not only visit her protege but also to visit Arcadia. Before long, Emily had convinced another person of the worth of her project and Stebbins and the association were soon involved in educating poor whites and blacks in the more isolated sections of the county. Although she was not aware of it at the time, Emily would soon be turning to Dow and Laura Stebbins for more immediate help in Heathsville.

As this pleasant summer began to draw to a close Emily's brief moment of happiness and fulfillment ended abruptly. She received news from home that her mother was critically ill and that Hannah's long years of suffering from an unknown disease were to end very shortly. After an unexplained delay Emily closed the school and traveled in what can be considered a leisurely pace to her mother's bedside in late August. Emily nursed her mother and cared for Slocum until Hannah died on September 3. Emily rarely mentioned positive feelings toward Hannah while she was alive; now with Hannah's death, Emily no longer wrote or spoke of her. If Emily was feeling great pain or loss for this final separation from Hannah, she confided these feelings to no one. Instead she wrote the obligatory thank you notes in response to condolences received and then continued on, picking up the threads of her briefly interrupted life.

With Hannah's death Emily felt that she had to make a painful choice between her father and Arcadia. She decided that her father, feeble and depressed in his bereavement, needed her more than the Northumberland people. Emily's friends and even her relatives acknowledged that her Arcadia project was "a noble mission." They assumed that her decision to remain with Slocum was a temporary one and that she would return to Virginia in the months to come.

Shortly after her mother's death Emily wrote to Dow and Stebbins requesting them to supervise her school and farm in her absence. They willingly agreed to this arrangement. She next recruited a young Quaker from neighboring Kings Ferry, New York, named Sarah Goodyear, to teach in her new schoolhouse while she directed the harvesting and planting via letter to Dow and Nash. She avidly followed every detail of rural life painted so vividly for her in letters from her Northumberland friends. While slipping quietly into her "new status as housekeeper & caretaker of dear father in his shady side of life, filling the place of her who is gone home in endless bliss," Emily's pen and mind were also involved in the political and social problems of Heathsville, Virginia.

It was rumored that the Bureau agent was misappropriating funds earmarked for education and relief. The Bureau's military leader stationed in Heathsville had become friendly with the county's leading ex-Confederate Democrat, Colonel Burgess, and fear that the freedmen's civil rights were now endangered was rampant. Emily's associates believed that corruption was commonplace within the Sixth District of the Bureau and Emily feared for the future of her tenants at Arcadia. She rented at no charge more five and ten acre plots to blacks who had been prevented from purchasing land. Her frequent letters to teachers and farmers were an attempt to keep morale high in her absence.

With the rise of the Ku Klux Klan in Heathsville and bitter fighting in progress between Democrats and Republicans over the adoption of the new Radical Republican state constitution, the situation for the county's blacks and Northern schoolteachers was becoming increasingly more uncomfortable as 1868 progressed. One year after Hannah Howland's death Caroline Putnam left Lottsburgh to visit Emily to persuade her to return to Heathsville. By the middle of October they were on their way. Arriving in Washington, Emily felt a special joy at being reunited with friends after the year's absence. Emma Brown, Colonel Folsom, the Dana's and the Bowens all made Howland's week in Washington a full and happy one. With more enthusiasm than she had felt since the previous summer she made the trip across the Potomac, arrived at her new house and settled down to put her Southern affairs in running order. Much to her surprise she found that Arcadia was successful and stable enough to function smoothly without her presence for long periods of time. Her worth to her project was fast becoming one of giving general direction, advice and morale. "The truth is my days fell into monotonous ways," Emily wrote to Hannah in December, 1868.

Colonel Folsom's name now began to appear in letters home. Emily had introduced Folsom to Miss Putnam and together they had worked to settle Putnam more comfortably into her new home before they returned to Washington. Folsom, taking Emily's advice not to conform to idle customs of society, offered his services to Carrie Putnam in the Holley School, thereby marking the beginning of a thirty-five year friendship. His admiration and respect for both Carrie and Emily is evident in his correspondence with Carrie. His feelings toward Emily were obviously deeper than admiration; for almost a two year period they carried on an unusual courtship. Although no direct evidence exists today that Folsom asked Emily to marry him, it can be assumed on the basis of their correspondence and Emily's diary in later years, that Folsom wished to marry her but that she refused him for reasons that she never clearly delineated. Emily's objections centered around how she viewed her self as a woman and the traditional role of married women in nineteenth century America. To be free to live as a feminist was of primary importance to her. Folsom, who fully supported reforms for black education and civil rights, was not sympathetic with her fight for the political and social equality of women. Another objection might have been Folsom's refusal to take the temperance pledge;

Emily was as unswerving in her adherence to the temperance cause as she was to the battle for freedmen's and women's rights.

They were two strong-minded people, single for over twenty years of their adult life, independent and stubborn holders of certain crucial opposing ideologies. Folsom, a landscape engineer in civilian life, was not a wealthy man and Emily's economic superiority may have been an additional factor in her refusal. She could be warm, expressive and loving but by the age of forty had learned to temper her emotions with calm reason and deliberate thought. Folsom and Emily parted civilly in 1869 although there most likely was some acrimony and regret on both sides. In a letter to Putnam, Folsom alluded to Emily's unfortunate inflexibility once she had made up her mind on a given subject. That same year Emily bitterly expressed her dissatisfaction with men's minds and natures in a letter to Emma Brown filled with advice against courtship and marriage.

Five years later Folsom unexpectedly resumed a correspondence with Emily which continued until his death in 1903. She was secretly pleased with this distant but friendly contact. They presented the merits of their respective causes and beliefs and intellectually battled with one another for the next thirty years. In an unusual move after his death, Emily had a water plant built at the Manassas Industrial School to be named in honor of Colonel Folsom. She also had his portrait painted to hang next to hers on the school room wall and traveled to Virginia at the age of seventy-seven to unveil them. Shortly before her death Emily remarked enigmatically to a friend that she wished that her friendship with Folsom might have been different.

In late 1868, however, Emily chose to make their relationship far different from the enigmatic and wistful thought she would hold in old age. Having rejected the opportunity to change and deepen her relationship with Folsom through marriage, she began to search for another path to growth.

PART II

Transition to a New World

Transition

The year 1869 was the setting for a number of random events in United States history: the passage of the Fifteenth Amendment granting suffrage to black men; the corrupt new Grant administration was in the White House; irresponsible entrepreneurs in the military-occupied Southern states; the advent of scandalous reconstruction Southern-state governments; an emerging split in the women's rights movement; and Radical Republicans reigning victorious in the halls of Congress. The epoch of Reconstruction had arrived but the ideal of the era—the binding up of the nation's wounds after the Civil War—was not apparent to many living in America in 1869.

The South lay in ruin after the Civil War. Severe economic and social dislocations resulting from the loss of manpower over the four years of the war had left their mark on the land and people. The financially bankrupt South faced not only a painful changeover from an economy based on slavery but also was suffering from the difficult psychological effects of their loss.

Reconstruction had begun auspiciously enough; loyal State governments in the South were established under President Andrew Johnson's plan. Southern senators and representatives were elected to Congress and the threatened penalties to the participants in the unsuccessful rebellion were surprisingly mild. As humanitarians sought to help the four million Southern blacks make the transition from slavery to freedom, women's rights movement leaders such as Elizabeth Cady Stanton, Lucretia Mott and Susan B. Anthony began to work once again for women's civil rights, hoping that this the Negro's Hour would also become the woman's hour.

But in three short years, this optimistic Reconstruction vision had faded. The shabby aspects of the era were too obvious and overshadowed the idealism too frequently to be ignored. The Radical Republicans, a powerful minority of Northerners, fought President Johnson's mild reconstruction plans. They repudiated "loyal" state governments established in the South and refused to seat Southern senators and representatives in Congress. After a year of bitter controversy, the Radicals succeeded in putting the South under military occupation, impeaching President Johnson, and coming within one vote of removing him from office.

These men held a vision of reforming Southern society based on a belief in the equality of the races. In 1868 their radical idealism was in part responsible for giving the blacks the equal protection of the law and citizenship. Yet these same Radicals were also in part responsible for allowing the perpetuation of corrupt carpetbagger state governments throughout the South. In the same year self-serving politicians and greedy, irresponsible entrepreneurs flourished in the climate set by the new Ulysses S. Grant administration with its scandals and its blatant prostitution of civil service. The nation's wounds were not being healed but were constantly ripped open by these political and economic abuses of power by men.

In 1868 two politically astute women had seen the potential for a further abuse of power by male politicians. When Elizabeth Cady Stanton and Susan B. Anthony read the wording of the Fourteenth Amendment, they recognized that the Radical Republicans were advocating *malehood* suffrage only and began working unsuccessfully to secure petitions against the amendment. They no longer naively believed that women were going to be rewarded the enfranchisement for their political, economic and humanitarian work during the Civil War. Many supporters in the women's rights movement had been involved in contributing to the Union cause and to the freedmen during the war, laying aside their own struggle to gain civil rights. Now in 1869, four years after the end of the war, these advocates of women's rights found themselves standing in either one of two camps. Lucy Stone and Julia Ward Howe and their followers advocated the passage of the Fourteenth and Fifteenth Amendment, feeling the question of sex was of lesser consideration and would endanger the chances of enfranchisement for male blacks. Stanton, Anthony and Lucretia Mott on the other hand refused to give up the opportunity to link women's suffrage with Negro enfranchisement. In May 1869 the split in the women's movement took place when Stanton and Anthony, calling for a women suffrage amendment to the Constitution, organized the National Women's Suffrage Association open to women only. Later that year, the American Women's Suffrage Association was established with Stone and Howe advocating their more conservative position. By this time the Fifteenth Amendment had been ratified and women would not gain the vote for another fifty years.

The hope that many women felt after experiencing new political, economic and social freedoms in roles brought about by the exigencies of wartime living began to disappear. The actual gains made by women politically as well as into the professions, trade unions, and higher education proved to be miniscule in the years following the close of the war.

For a small group of women, however, the beginning of Reconstruction did not mean an end to their unusual war-related roles. These women, rather than returning to their Northern homes, continued to work as missionaries and teachers in the South on behalf of the freedmen. By their geographic distance alone they were removed from the battle raging around women and black suffrage and from the continued discrimination against women in the professions and education.

Emily Howland, in 1869, found herself moving from this more isolated position in the South into the world of social concerns, conflicting political ideologies and problematic positions centered on the role of women in the industrial North. Emily held strong ties of friendship with women in both the National and American Women Suffrage Associations. She had spent the last seven years of her life helping black men and women break the psychological and intellectual chains placed on them in their slavery bondage. Her twin concerns throughout the past two decades had been abolitionism and women's rights. Although eschewing higher education for herself, she had been sponsoring college training for both black and white women throughout the 1860s. In returning to Sherwood, New York Emily was entering a world far different than the one she had left to work in the South. Women's rights advocates were no longer united and Emily would have to choose her position on the emerging radical-conservative continuum.

She had been immersed in the world of the freedmen and their economic and political plight. Now she found herself confronted with new questions and new solutions about her commitment to feminism on a personal as well as political level. Women's future was no longer connected to the fate of the freedmen. Her twin concerns for equal rights for blacks and women were separate and Emily had to decide to which she would pay primary allegiance.

Just twelve years earlier she had written that letter to her mother seeking to leave the safety of her home and family to venture forth in a new and alien world. Now she was returning to Sherwood but her Northern home no longer represented a safe or familiar haven. Her mother was dead. Her brothers lived in separate homes with their

growing families. Her Philadelphia network was scattered throughout the states and Europe. Most important, her present ideology had
evolved and grown in accord with her life in the freedmen's world,
not apace with the rapidly changing Northern society. Emily now
found herself in the unique position once again of venturing forth
into a new world. This time it was called Sherwood, New York.

*Slocum Howard, Emily and Grant on the verandah at Tanglewild, the
Howland residence in Sherwood, New York. (Courtesy Friends Historical
Library of Swarthmore College)*

6

The Physical Odyssey Ends

In the final days of 1868 Emily Howland decided to bring to an end the physical and ideological odyssey into the freedmen's world that began eleven years earlier when she left Sherwood to teach at Myrtilla Miner's school. She had experienced new thoughts and ideas, traveling to a world far different from rural Sherwood and had immersed herself in the range of emotions and conflicts associated with friendship, death, mourning and her own sexuality. She had lost both her mother and her adopted daughter. Also she had maintained her independence by rejecting a relationship with a man she respected and by keeping her distance in relating to her female friends. As winter approached, Emily began to struggle to close out not one but many chapters in her life opened during the past eleven years. She now was ending her commitment to build a new, visionary community in rural Virginia. For the first time Emily felt truly alone.

She had rejected the life of the reformer, the intellectual, the Quaker minister, wife, mother, now the philanthropist. Not certain where to turn, unsure of herself, Emily decided to retreat to the comfort, security and love to be found with Slocum in her family home in Sherwood. She no longer wished to embark on arduous physical journeys as in the past, yet she knew that she was not ready to deal with that metaphysical odyssey necessary for growth and change as an individual. At the age of forty-one, Emily was uncertain how to proceed with turning inward in search of self. The next two years would be spent trying on and discarding roles which would allow her the freedom to better understand herself and accept much of what she discovered.

The year 1869 marks Emily's first full-fledged attempt in self-discovery. She tried to lead a quiescent life at her home in Sherwood, New York, giving herself many needed hours to reflect on her life past, present and future. She neither traveled for pleasure nor toiled for reform but continued to remain in Sherwood at her father's side. She was now solely responsible for the efficient management of his household since Hannah and William had moved to their own home one quarter mile west of the Corners on the Ridge Road.

She soon became restless and discontent with this return to an essentially domestic role. She struggled with but could not make a successful transition from Reconstruction reformer to rural domestic in so short a time. Emily acknowledged being tied by invisible bonds to her father yet she was clearly unhappy with this voluntary form of enslavement. Incapable of leaving him, dissatisfied with a non-activist role and discouraged with her attempts to understand herself better, Emily found neither peace nor fulfillment in her return home.

Emily's relationship with Slocum Howland became increasingly important to her, compensating emotionally for the losses she had experienced the previous autumn and for the discouragement she currently felt. Her father soon became her favorite topic of discussion with her female friends during this year. When Emily enthusiastically supported Cornelia Hancock's new plan to model a colony on Cat Island, South Carolina after her Arcadia, the two women began to seek ways to enlist Slocum's financial and moral support in this venture. As Slocum became involved, agreeing with their plans and underwriting the colony financially, Cornelia wrote to Emily, "I think thy father's kindness in helping my enterprise along is the outgrowth of a *very strong affection for thee.* I think he has read thy desire in the matter and has silently concluded it should be done to help on thy abiding love for these people. Of course I don't know him but this seems the way to me. Write me something of him, tell me if I am not right in this. I don't mean to suppose he is not interested in the cause." Cornelia's opinion of her relationship with her father pleased Emily and she soon was sharing more information about the most important male in her life.

These two women touched upon more than familial relationships and their concern for Southern black education, however. Cornelia repeatedly returned to the theme of role alternatives for single women in their Southern work. "I am so impressed with the feeling it is such a sphere of usefulness open for single women to come among and be eyes, ears and understanding for these people for a time," Cornelia told Emily. This may have been a painful subject for Emily since she had rejected this type of role for herself after her mother's death. But her written response to such statements reflected only her insistence that her time of work with blacks was now over. Yet certain of her actions belie her written response. Home in Sherwood only a few months Emily began to make plans to educate black females from Arcadia in New York. This plan reflects the still unresolved conflict Emily felt in choosing her father over Arcadia. By educating these young women at the neighboring Union Springs school run by Emily's relative Robert Howland while having them live at her father's home Emily could carry out both her duty to her father and to her people in Arcadia. In late spring Sidney the first young woman arrived in Sherwood to work and live at the Howland home and be educated at Robert Howland's school. In a letter later that year to Carrie Putnam Emily discussed her domestic training and formal education project in glowing terms. Her initial plans had grown to new proportions for she began to envision Sidney and later recruits as the new educators of the colony. Upon their return to Arcadia they would be well-prepared to function as model teachers, mothers and wives. Emily continued to center on fostering black competency rather than on aggrandizing herself by inducing their dependence on her. Indeed the very fragility of her commitment or her personal ability to keep it may have made her the more sensitive to training them to do without her.

Activities relating to this plan were not enough however to satisfy Emily's latent reformist needs. As cold winter weather settled in her thoughts turned repeatedly to the South. Her father had remained healthy since her return home and appeared to be in good spirits, prompting Emily to feel that perhaps she could leave him for a short visit to Acadia. "Discouragement is a state of mind we all have enough of, I fancy for our good," she wrote Hannah in explaining her departure from Sherwood. She discovered that she could not rid herself of feeling that she "had been led thither to be put through the wilderness of Virginia for some cause, to make it blossom as the rose." No longer able to justify staying with Slocum constantly when he was in good health and since she could not convince him to return to Virginia with her, Emily journeyed alone to Northumberland and loosened bonds she had helped forge over the past year.

In contrast with her last visit shortly after her mother's death, Emily no sooner arrived than her services were demanded from a number of different quarters. The blacks in Arcadia as well as in neighboring areas were in need of clothing and farming equipment. Once again, she wrote letters to friends and relatives begging for their cast-off clothes and tools. She was pleased with the work of the schools and teachers in and around Heathsville and found herself particularly proud of the quality of education provided by the Howland School under the guidance of her New York friend and former neighbor Sarah Goodyear.

Less than a month after her arrival in Virginia, Emily sent a message to her father saying that she had unexpectedly been asked to start a new school in Westmoreland County, Virginia. She wrote requesting his permission to remain for three more months to set up the school. Although forty-two years old, Emily continued to seek parental consent before undertaking a new project. The struggle within Emily to achieve a sense of autonomy continued, pointing to the confusion Emily felt in handling her position as unmarried daughter and dependent within the family.

Slocum did not answer the letter but had his niece Sarah Alsop who was caring for him in Emily's absence write his thoughts on the matter. His disappointment and disapproval of her plans is evident. "I have asked him what I must write and he says, 'Well, let her do as she has a mind to if she thinks best to stay let her do it.' Now all I will say can thee afford to be away from him so long." Emily felt that she could; she moved to Kinsale, Westmoreland County in January after dividing more lots of land at Arcadia for new families and building a teacher's home.

In a letter to an aunt, Emily described the need for a colony like Arcadia in this new county but did not state her official position or relationship with either the government or relief agencies. The government was paying for the construction of her school but if Howland was being paid for her teaching services, she did not record it. Within a week, she began to detail her "specific work here beside the school . . . Since coming here and learning the frauds and extortions practiced on the people, I see it has been a great benefit to them for land to be owned in their midst—held for them to buy at fair price & sure title." Emily continued to see the new, relatively powerless, planter class as the oppressors and felt that at least one farm like Arcadia in every county "would be a great check on the wicked wills of the old slavocracy, who let no whit of a chance to oppress escape them."

As the first phase of Radical Reconstruction came to a close Emily no longer felt as though she understood all that was taking place in rural Virginia. Within one year the situation had changed considerably. "We have all been feeling keenly anxious, all loyal people white & col'd—in regard to our future" she remarked to a New York relative. She predicted melodramatically that "If Va was restored to the Union with universal amnesty and suffrage, martyrdom & flight would be the fate of the loyal (Union) people" for "the prospect of restored power makes these rebels hating & fierce at once. Still the state of fear here is something we can scarcely understand." The seeds of hating and fear that were to erupt in violence and force, collapsing the Radical Southern governments during the mid-70s, were being sown in these rural Virginia counties at the close of this tumultuous decade.

Emily planned to stay until she felt her work in Westmoreland County was finished satisfactorily. She had not found a replacement to take over her teaching duties as she had promised her father when requesting three months additional leave from Sherwood. In letters from her fellow teachers at Arcadia, no mention of Emily's work as being temporary was ever made. Thus when Emily returned to Sherwood at the end of February in answer to a summons to nurse her sick father it came as a surprise to her Virginia colleagues.

Her return to New York effectively marks the end of any long-term intensely emotional involvement with the rural Virginia black communities and their concerns. She would continue to support Arcadia financially when necessary and to sell the land to the tenants for fair price on request. She would also continue to pay the teacher's salary at the Howland School in Heathsville as well as the expenses for supplies and building maintenance well into the twentieth century. At least ten young women from the county were educated at the Howland Seminary in Union Springs, and perhaps a half dozen more received college degrees from Howard University and Oberlin through Emily Howland's financial support. Each of these actions attests to Emily's interest in the future welfare of the black women and men of the county. Yet these actions were emotionally distant, requiring little personal contact and involvement in the lives of individual blacks on Emily's part and most important little deviation from the traditional role of domesticity. With her call to attend to her father's needs, Emily stopped being the "eyes, ears and understanding for these people." Leaving their world she retreated into the closed rural community of Sherwood making only brief periodic visits to Virginia.

This time Emily's return was permanent. She had made a temporary commitment to reform in 1870 but the ties to her father pulled her back to Sherwood. 1869 may have been a year of inward struggle for Emily but 1870 represents the year in which she waged a definitive battle with herself. She had pitted her love for her father against her love of Arcadia, domesticity against activism and familial responsibility against her duties to the Philadelphia group and to herself. The results of this psychological war heralded the beginning of a decade which was to be filled with bitterness, unhappiness, conflict, doubt and despair for Emily. Pain, problems, frustration and joy became her daily companions as she tried to come to terms with her complex feelings, needs and desires. She knew that she had a far more arduous journey ahead of her than the one she faced in 1857, yet she did not retreat. She turned inward and now faced the difficult terrain of the mind rather than that of geographic space.

7

Cat in a Strange Garret

June 1, 1873 dawned clear and dry, promising to be one of those warm sparkling days found frequently in late spring in central New York. As the day ran its course the good weather continued, energizing people and reminding them of the miracle of rebirth taking place around them.

As this day ended a forty-four year old woman sat at her dining room table with a diary in her hand. In sharp contrast with the beauty and joy outside, she began to write words of unhappiness and self-deprecation. As Emily Howland pushed the thick grey and brown hair away from her round gentle face she told that old confidant, her diary: "I feel like a cat in a strange garret."

Her strange garret was Sherwood, New York where her position both in her father's home and within the Friends community left so many of her needs unfulfilled. Yet she willingly made the choice to pass her time in this strange garret, drawn by love to her father and sense of duty and responsibility to his welfare. Emily knew that she was paying for this choice dearly and this entry was part of the intense psychic suffering that had begun earlier.

Her father had recovered from his February, 1870 illness and although enfeebled by advancing old age, he remained healthy enough over the years to walk daily to his store managed by William Howland. He continued to participate in the Orthodox Friends meetings for business and worship, and in his quiet, gentle manner sought to open the lines of communication between the four branches of

Friends in the Sherwood vicinity. It must be assumed that his tolerance for others' beliefs and opinions extended to include those of his
daughter Emily. At no time in the 1870's does Emily note a difference of opinion or open conflict with her father. Instead their relationship from Emily's perspective appears to have pivoted around
Emily's maternal ministrations to Slocum. She nursed him through
illnesses; worried about his health, appetite, appearance and dress;
was anxious about his well-being when he was away from the home
and fretted over him when he was with her. In one typical week's
entries in the beginning of the decade such phrases of concern
include "I troubled about father because he was more thinly clad
than usual," "I fitted fa. off for mtg.," "I worry about father" and
"No father yet." That same week she noted her newfound responsibility of washing and ironing his shirts, leaving the rest of the laundry in the hands of Sidney, the Arcadian. She bought Slocum's
clothes, mended and cleaned them and managed the family's household finances and domestic help. Without entering into a marriage
Emily was slipping into the traditional maternal-domestic role which
with pain, confusion and disapproval she had once rejected. In fact

*Tanglewild, Emily Howland's home in Sherwood, New York. (Courtesy
Friends Historical Library of Swarthmore College)*

she now consciously assumed the responsibility of both mothering an aged parent and running a large home constantly filled with her father's friends and relatives.

Emily's immersion in the cult of domesticity was acknowledged by her associates as well during the early part of the decade. In the fall of 1871 Margaret Burleigh made a remarkable request of Emily, asking her to take on the responsibility of caring for a twenty-eight year old English ex-convict named Edward Strange. He was dying from tuberculosis with no friends or relatives in the States to care for him other than Grew, Burleigh and their network. Since Emily was the only unmarried member exclusively involved with maternal-domestic concerns, Burleigh logically turned to her for help. The network felt that Strange had been the helpless and unfortunate product of a poor home environment and that his larceny was the result of both his lack of family life and the unenlightened penal systems here and in England. Taking their cue from the penal reformers of the day they felt that with a loving religious environment and proper medical treatment, his rehabilitation both physically and psychologically would occur. Burleigh thought that this project would also prove to be therapeutic for Emily in her battle to overcome her recurring depressions and negative self-image. When Strange arrived at the Sherwood house Emily responded in a maternal manner to him, trying to build up his strength, driving him to visit friends, relatives and to meetings, reading to him and holding long discussions on moral and philosophical issues. Significantly Emily commented on their growing friendship by saying that he now "lives on friendly terms with a cat." This is one of the many times during this period in which she used a cat to describe herself. Felines historically have been associated with the female sex—a connection with both positive and negative connotations. The cat has been seen as independent, emotionally distant, intelligent, manipulative, associated with supernatural powers, loving and loyal only to a rare circle. Unfortunately, Emily did not share why she chose the cat as a symbol. We can only assume that some of these characteristics appeared appropriate to her.

Edward Strange became bedridden in mid-winter and Emily nursed him constantly, providing another maternal outlet to this unmarried woman. When the inevitable death watch began, Emily wrote "I feel so happy to have him a little longer. I fancy I must seem like a mother whose baby is taken from her. He has been my chief thought and care for nearly 6 months. It is terribly hard rending the tie." He died three days after Emily wrote this and due to inclement weather his body remained in the house for a week before the burial in the Howland family cemetery could take place. This delay caused Emily and Slocum additional emotional upset and heightened Emily's sense of loss and her grief. A month after Strange died Burleigh wrote a worried letter to Emily attempting to help her cope with the fact of his death. Emily evidently had expressed, to a disturbing extent, her depression, pain and self-hatred. "Little woman, I want thee to be more merciful to mine Emilie," Burleigh began. "She is a dear good woman & I can't have her blamed for the lack of infinite powers. Come now, I have constituted myself her physician & thou must take heed of my advice. I must not speak thus of one who is sick at heart, but must encourage her to cleanse the full bosom of that perilous stuff. And to whom better than to her doctor? All winter I rejoiced that the mother love in thee was so beautifully brought into blossom . . . We know that under the happy influences of the last ½ year he made some progress, and now all is so happily ended, do rejoice with me." In trying to comfort Emily, Burleigh managed to strike at the heart of Emily's depression when she perceived it to be more than mourning for Strange, her second surrogate child to die. Burleigh felt that Emily's dangerous psychological state was caused in part by the separation from the Philadelphia network and by the quality of her relationship with Slocum. "The one thing I lament is the loneliness which lets thy power of loving wear upon thyself instead of blessing others and thyself. From the time I resolved to go to Charleston, (to visit Cornelia Hancock) my mind was otherwise occupied. Would that thee had the same opportunity of recovering equanimity."

If Emily were to live with this choice of remaining with Slocum then all Burleigh felt she could do was warn her not to strive "to make her pint pot hold a quart." Burleigh begged her to join the network physically once again so that they could take over the familial duty of caring for her lovingly since now "there's nobody to take care of thee & thee has no capacity to take care of thyself." Posing a series of revealing questions, Burleigh asked her: "How if quite disabled from ministering to thy father's wants? How if thee grew worrisome or gloomy with the life which does not sufficiently nourish thy soul or give scope to thy activity? Will is not enough, soul and body have their needs which must not be too long withstood." Once again Emily summarily rejected this beloved friend's advice and remained at her father's side, denying those "needs of her body and soul."

By May, essentially without the network's help, Emily had come to terms with her grief. Although death "looks very sad, I notice that most things seemingly sad are most fruitful & beneficient—cloudy rainy days—how depressing & dreary yet the fountains whence spring life & beauty. So I dread death no more. It must lead to a larger life." Later that month, she reflected further on the nature of her mourning. "How strange is the going over of such a wound. At first all sense is permeated with the loss. Little by little this lessens. Soon it no longer absorbs but becomes one of the experiences of life." This quiet understanding and acceptance of death and mourning was to remain with Emily Howland until the time of her own death fifty years later.

A quiet acceptance of death did not mean however that Emily was free of those depressions which arose, as Burleigh so correctly analyzed, from her Sherwood environment. Extended "invalid" physical and emotional states lasting up to six weeks would occur in her life on a cyclical basis. These physically and mentally debilitating periods would appear in the latter part of winter and again in the early fall throughout this decade. These states coincided with her return from visits with friends in Philadelphia, Virginia and South Carolina—all part of her extended Philadelphia group. While away from Sherwood her only depressed notations referred to her anticipated homecoming: "I dread to go home so much I wish I could be set down there without any volition." reads a typical end-of-visit entry.

Shorter periods of depression ranging from two days to a week, accompanied by bitter self-abnegation, occur on a less systematic calendar basis. However, patterns emerge when these less prolonged states of depression are given a second look. When correspondence from a member of the Philadelphia network was received or a visit from a member had concluded or was deferred, Emily's depression was noted immediately thereafter in almost every case. She usually felt a need "to exorcise this sense of neither being needed or wanted anywhere." Viewing her sense of duty as slumbering she compared her life in Sherwood to prolonged hibernation in which she was offered only "glimpses of self which I despise!" At these times Emily found her associates in Cayuga County neither interesting, refined nor cultured and longed for a visit from one of the network.

In the months following Strange's death, Emily had made an attempt however to turn to the slow rhythm of her Sherwood life "content to grow old (for) I have lived a long time." She had seriously misjudged both her longevity and her contentment. By late summer, 1872 wave after wave of depression and self-abnegation unrelated to mourning had begun to sweep over her. She had been proud of the fact that she had earned and received wages during the war, in Northumberland County and teaching French in Sherwood in 1871. She knew that she was capable of earning her living if given the chance but could not even prove herself in this way any longer. She saw or imagined other facets of her character which did not please her and robbed her of her self-esteem. Life at these times ran "low & bitter & black," with "mud & snow beneath, clear sky & sunshine above like all the rest of life, wallowing in drudgery & pettiness with a head as far from it as the furthest star." Emily clearly saw her maternal-domestic role in Sherwood as sheer drudgery with relief coming only in the form of intellectual pursuits. When an elderly female neighbor died while ironing Emily tersely commented with an odd blend of sarcasm and wistfulness "Died in the harness at 88, who would not wish to go thus?" After spring cleaning for two weeks Emily feared that "in time I could become a hum-drum drudge so fully occupied with trying to keep clean & in order as to know or care for little else . . . but my better part revolts from becoming thus absorbed and I shall not."

Interestingly enough, Emily realized for the first time the full extent of the childbearing, rearing and homemaking responsibilities carried by the nineteenth century woman. "I think how many poor women have such heavy burdens whose strength is quite unequal to it. There can be no cheerful working when one almost totters with weakness." She lamented frequently that "the body seems so puny and the work so hard & tedious, after working a few hours I always feel as tho' I am being used up to little purpose." She found herself sewing more frequently, using these times as "resting spells." Such a routine led her to sarcastically compare the homemakers' lot with that of the work horse for "they both draw blind" as they go about their daily activities. Not surprisingly Howland found herself longing for rest, ease and intellectual stimulation and growth. The only way she could imagine rising out of the black, bitter despair was by coveting a new kind of life which she was afraid her move to Sherwood had placed permanently beyond her grasp. "I want to read, everything moves me—my thirst for knowledge was never so strong—but eyes fail & work must be done."

The only times she surfaced from under the waves of her depression would be for those few free minutes when she could teach herself a new intellectual skill such as the study of entomology or illuminating. She admitted that she was most "cheerful only when I can mix Emily Howland's with plenty of others' thoughts."

Yet, increasingly burdensome household tasks continued to interfere with her intellectual development, Similarly, the demands arising from her relationship with Slocum continued to disrupt her pursuit of an intellectual way of life. The maternal-domestic aspects of this unusual father-daughter relationship did not interfere with Slocum's assertion of his parental right to direct and control Emily's life in a number of significant ways. Although Emily felt that her father in childhood had raised her with a "wholesome letting alone," in later years Slocum seems to have subtly manipulated Emily's life. Burleigh had perceived Emily as being in many ways the willing subordinate partner in an unequal relationship with Slocum, experiencing a loss of autonomy, freedom and mobility in her love for her father. Her depressions and struggles were seen as reactions to her need to experience more independence, self-control and decision-making power than their relationship permitted. Emily to a large extent was growing aware of these damaging and conflicting psychological processes in operation but in the first half of the decade did little to alleviate her psychic suffering through change.

A relatively minor but representative case in point can be found in May, 1873. "I wanted to go to the woods with the young people but Father took a fancy to go to Augustus Howland's so I could not." Rather than seek aggressively to change her male-defined and regulated life, Emily instead turned inward and passively withdrew into intellectual pursuits with the comment "Pacified myself easily with reading." When Slocum insisted on sending Phebe Wood, a relative and Emily's confidant at this time, home after a prolonged visit Emily's response was twofold and immediate, an increase in the number of letters sent to the members of the Philadelphia group and Virginia friends and the reading of the seven hundred page feminist novel *Middlemarch* by George Eliot.

Not surprisingly Emily became depressed after such episodes and in her diary made eloquent pleas for more leisure, privacy and the right to "enjoy the company of those I like." Rather than seeking out such company she continued to turn increasingly inward and toward domesticity, taking on the family's sewing as well as laundry tasks. This last task proved too much for her however and she turned unexpectedly and fiercely upon this expression of the cult of domesticity for robbing her of her escape through reading. When Phebe Wood and Anna Searing visited to cheer her up, Emily found that even they could not rid her of feeling "thoroughly jaded body & mind" and "insupportable to myself." As the depression intensified, she could only bring herself to write "I am but a limp rag across the grain of things." Frequently Emily would juxtapose the passive and the aggressive in a mixed metaphor to describe the paradoxical non-resisting yet irritating aspects of her own behavior and interpersonal relations.

Emily soon began to weave her religious ideas and experiences in with her depressions and negative self-image. Gradually, she convinced herself that her fellow Friends in Sherwood regarded her in a singularly negative light. Although disliking being labeled deviant, she nevertheless continued to avoid attending meetings for worship and business and let it be known that she preferred to use quiet during the Quaker First Day meeting time to read, write and contemplate rather than to sit in silent worship at the meeting house. She openly questioned the merits of evangelism, revivals, a literal interpretation of the Bible and regular attendance at church services. When one of her neighbors, William Empson, gave her a copy of Headley's *Women of the Bible* to read she admitted that Empson thought her "in a dangerous state spiritually." Paradoxically, although she expected her unorthodox religious actions to merit such responses by the community she was nevertheless distressed when they did occur. Emily however did not alter her behavior in the slightest, preferring to once again liken herself to a cat in unfamiliar territory. Emily knew full well the determinative effect her religious actions had upon the type and quality of her relations with both family and neighbors. In disregarding the self-imposed censure of being labeled different Emily was now ready to follow a solitary path.

Strangely enough Slocum obviously either had no control or did not wish to exert overt control over Emily's lack of participation in Friendly activities. Slocum may not have understood his daughter's religious attitudes and found comfort in reverting back to his policy of "a wholesome letting alone" in this matter. It was at this time that Emily wrote in her diary that her relative Robert Howland, not Slocum, had now become "the only person who has breadth enough to comprehend or judge my views fairly." This entry points to a significant development in Emily's interpersonal relations in Sherwood during the early part of this decade; Emily's growing alienation and estrangement from both her father and her community resulted in the labeling of Emily as different, unorthodox and peculiar by the community and, more important, by Emily herself.

On the other hand, Emily viewed the Friends in a highly positive manner after comparing them with other religious groups on the basis of spiritually and social concerns—a comparison which only served to further underscore her own sense of deviance. She felt that the Friends "mean well & will do good" but she was nevertheless fearful of "making a bad & probably incorrect impression" upon them in an attempt to express her views. She held a continuing debate with herself as she struggled to resolve this identity problem. She finally acknowledged that the only solution for the present was to consider herself *with* the Friends but not one *of* them. With this rejection of one aspect of community life she had taken another step in her withdrawal from the world around her. She began to analyze herself and in her descriptions she used fewer mixed aggressive/passive metaphors and became increasingly hostile. It seems strange, even at this distance, to read the often tormented and aggressive words of this seemingly mild-mannered, middle-aged woman. "Alas there is so much unconquered savagery here within. I seem to only seduce the borders," reads one such telling phrase in her diary.

This withdrawal only served to increase Emily's sense of loneliness. Her isolation continued unabated and unrelieved except for her rare brief winter visits to her friends in Philadelphia and Virginia. During the middle years of the decade her life appears to have followed a discernable pattern—depression, negative self-image, withdrawal, loneliness, brief respite which temporarily broke the cycle, re-entry into the Sherwood community followed by yet another depression. Her view of the world and her problems coping with her environment remained essentially unchanged. She continued to dichotomize her life between a longing for knowledge and the unpleasant reality of familial duties and responsibilities. Her depressions were as frequent and as debilitating as earlier in the decade while her position within the community remained as marginal as ever.

Emily next made attempts to delineate her "hungering for something beyond" and intertwined this longing in her recurring litany of trial, doubt and despair. Commenting upon her brother Benjamin's similar depressions, Emily perhaps projected the cause of her own unhappiness upon him with her sympathetic exclamation, "What burdens we do bind to ourselves which can never be unbound in this life." Did choosing to stay with her father until his death lay at the root of her pathos?

After the age of 43, she often used imagery that dealt with coldness, numbness and life-suspension when in such restless, hungering moods. In one of her more revealing entries she brought in a favorite image when she compared herself to a diseased Christmas rose. "I thought why can't I rise from the freezing into life & the kind of beauty I am capable of. Suppose many of the petals of my being are blighted by the frost & snow of time and trial. Have I not something of worth left? My buds like those who have left the chill may never open; still remembering what they have endured in the icy embrace of winter, their life & beauty is more remarkable than all the glow of a garden in summertime."

Emily's depressions seem far more complex than a direct reaction to the narrow role imposed upon her by living with Slocum in Sherwood. Strangely enough, after each letter from Colonel Charles W. Folsom, her depressions became acute. At times she fought with herself for days whether she should continue the correspondence which was both painful and pleasant. It was only during the years that Emily can be assumed to have been going through menopause that this conflicting painful-pleasant reaction and subsequent depression can be found. In light of the above passage on the Christmas rose, Folsom's letters may have heightened for Emily the significance of the end of her childbearing years. Folsom more than any other male could awaken her to the full loss which she may have felt when faced with the finality of her reproductive functioning. His contact with her during these years if viewed in these terms would only serve to deepen her sense of depression and self-deprecation.

It is possible that Emily did not marry Folsom or any man because she felt it would interfere with her involvement in the Philadelphia network. If this had been a factor in her decision, during the 1870s Emily may have felt her loss of the network in the same vein as her physical sterility. Lending credence to this conjecture is that Emily not only viewed herself at this time as a non-functioning member of this activist group but also insisted on stressing a sterile, isolated and non-productive image of herself when communicating with these friends. Menopause for Emily may have meant facing the cruel irony of her double loss: her sterility in both traditional and non-traditional roles.

Certainly, hormonal changes took place but Emily at no time discussed the physical aspects of menopause. Instead she viewed herself as a tree that had the potential but never bore fruit; as a bud which never flowered; as an infinitely sad and mysterious person who might still prosper without attaining natural motherhood. "Vulgar sadness someone calls this depression without cause. Why suffer so much for what seems mistakes now. They may not be at all." She may have been referring to the finality which menopause heralds—a state which was traditionally greeted with happiness by married women in the nineteenth century. Unfortunately little has been written from the single woman's perspective, and few contemporary accounts of unmarried women's responses to menopause exist.

In the midst of depression she may have bitterly regretted her unmarried status and non-motherhood. In less depressed moments however she reverted to her long-held belief in the superiority of single life for women. "I had the pleasure of mtg M.H. . . . who will not lower her ideals to enter the estate of matrimony," she wrote on one occasion. On another her immediate response to the death of a young friend was "Oh how sad if Susy has given her life for motherhood."

In 1877 Emily reached the age of fifty. In this same year, minor distinctions in her rotation through her cycles of depression appeared. Her reading program of study and correspondence with the network occupied increasingly large portions of her day. She allowed day help to carry more of the domestic burden. Her father was mentioned less often and with less anxiety. More important, she was beginning to write about areas of interest other than her continual self-analysis. Social concerns began to replace personal introspection, heralding perhaps the end of this introspective period in her life.

This is not to say that some of the old devils did not continue to plague her. A theme of desperate isolation, of an inability to reach other people, of monotony and despair still dominated certain days and weeks. Phrases such as "never felt so alone in my life," "I am slowly growing away from everyone," "changes which terrify me are coming over my character," remained never far from her thoughts. By the last half of the decade, however, she began to lay to rest some of these devils in an increasingly different and more effective manner. Before, she had withdrawn, taking no direction other than a self-destructive introspection.

In 1877, Emily adopted two approaches to attain better mental health. She constructed a highly positive, coherent "fantasy world" in which she could retreat from the psychic pain arising out of her untenable domestic role. This fantasy world was not that of the psychotic where the individual loses contact with reality. Hers was a healthful, non-pathological mechanism for meeting the demands of life in Sherwood and her ego needs as well. Books, periodicals, and correspondence took on an additional dimension and constituted a fantasy world which in time of need would become more important to her than the primary relationships faced in Sherwood on a day-to-day basis. She would not move herself physically from Sherwood, New York but she did travel vicariously into different times and places with her favorite escapist literature—novels, travel, guides and histories. Books on French and German grammar, botany, political economy, entomology, illuminating and painting took her beyond the confines of her village. Mazzini and Plato were more real to her in September 1878 than many members of her nuclear and extended family or her neighbors in Sherwood. She spoke of the writers in the *Woman's Journal, Harpers* and the *New Republic* as one would of close friends.

Her correspondence, always voluminous, also held an increasingly important position in her life. Her communication with the beloved Philadelphia group appears to have been the second successful technique for coping with her Sherwood life. Her psychological life was a burdensome, pressured, non-autonomous yet paradoxically self-directed and self-imposed regime. "I try to do right," "I must," "I should," "I don't sally with intuition," "I have sad discouraged tho'ts when not intensely busy," "I should feel . . .," "I strain with my might" are all frequently repeated phrases in Howland's letters. Her dedication to performing endless duties, responsibilities and tasks was now recognized, mentioned and approved by members of the Philadelphia network who happened to be similarly motivated. Emily herself even attributed her depressions in part to the difference between the quality of her duties and those acted upon by her reformist-intellectual friends.

Referring to her slumbering sense of duty she berated herself for her lack of substantial reformist or intellectual activities. Her Philadelphia friends reminded her that she was already staggering under self-imposed familial and community responsibilities in Sherwood and gently gave her the support she needed. These letters enriched her world considerably as she received the friendship and intellectual stimulation she craved.

All of this is not to say that Emily was friendless in Sherwood. On the contrary, she did have a number of men and women with whom she associated daily and spent a small portion of her time visiting. In a typical week at the end of November, 1877 she had visited with or was visited by members of thirteen neighboring families or relatives. The distinction that Emily made here was that the members of the Philadelphia group were a vital network with whom she shared a strong bond of friendship, love, social concerns, and support different from that shared with isolated individuals within the Sherwood community. Hannah Letchworth Howland was perhaps Emily's closest friend as well as relative, yet Emily never attempted to integrate Hannah into her reformer-intellectual Philadelphia network. Emily did receive emotional support and at times was emotionally dependent upon Hannah and a handful of other women living in western New York, notably Charlotte Pearl and Laura Searing, two Sherwood homemakers; Dr. Amanda Sanford, one of the first women graduates of the University of Michigan Medical School; and Phebe Coffin, an Auburn teacher and far less radical relative of Lucretia Coffin Mott and Martha Coffin Wright. But these friendships were strictly one-to-one relationships with no bonds tying these women together as a group. No New York network formed around Emily nor did she become a member of a group that had either the depth or complexity of interrelations and purposes of the Philadelphia women. Emily remained kind, interested but personally aloof and emotionally distant from most of her neighbors and friends.

She developed as a coping technique the ability to distance herself from her Sherwood neighbors and friends by assuming a friendly but impenetrable mask. No longer did she act out her discontent through overtly deviant behavior which had, in turn, reaffirmed her own self-hatred. Now she used her diaries, correspondence and reading as a form of self-expression, leaving her personal relations superficial and untroubled. In her writing she could release her bitterness, despair, conflicts, problems and doubts in a less emotionally charged, if not distancing manner. By such techniques she could break the cycle of dependency upon the community for her total image feedback. Furthermore, participation based upon emotional non-involvement rather than overt withdrawal from community activities was a viable alternative which would diminish the incidence of being negatively viewed by Friends and extended family. She began to attend community meetings more frequently but refused to embrace the beliefs, practices and goals of the different groups with the fervor she previously applied to her group commitments.

In a letter to her mother years earlier Emily had remarked that "the less visiting the less danger of quarreling & that is the besetment of relatives or of people much alike living near. There is scarce a family in our circle that is exactly pleasant to mention the others in, yet they are all good people, only too comfortable, too wealthy & too near together." Her view of the community and relatives had not changed appreciably in 1878. In becoming a participating yet emotionally marginal member, she felt she had found a solution to her continual problem of coping with close family and community relations.

On one level this approach proved highly successful for she began to receive positive community feedback. Her obvious distance was perceived by both family and neighbors as a sign of strength and resourcefulness and they soon began to consider her as a dominant community leader rather than an emotionally estranged woman in their midst. More and more frequently she was asked to speak at many of the lcoal and county reform society meetings. In response to one such request she felt that she had to justify this new role to her niece Isabel, saying that she felt in recent times "bound to speak any word for a good cause which I am asked for."

At least twice a year, the men in her community sought her advice regarding care of the local cemetery. Later in the decade she was elected Worthy Chief of the local temperance lodge and commented typically that it was "against my own wishes. I dread it." But she accepted that as well as other community honors. The Cayuga County Historical Society asked her to present a paper to their group on the history of the early Friends in the county, feeling she was the best representative of the Friends in the area. Her modest response was that her "essay was as much praised as I dispraised it & I went home relieved that it was all over."

She reluctantly assumed this highly visible public role within the community though the irony of the situation did not escape her. She found herself however becoming more occupied with changes taking place within her own family than with her relationship with the community. As her father became less mobile and more easily fatigued Emily began to take over duties Slocum had considered predominantly male in nature. By the late 1870s Emily virtually had control of the family's substantial finances, was loaning money, extending credit, and overseeing the farms under her family's management. She did not assume however any of the responsibility for her father's store or interests in local mills; this was under the care of her older brother William. Both William and her younger brother Benjamin came to her with their business problems, as did other men and women from the Sherwood area. It was not unusual to find a ncighbor visiting Emily seeking advice about proper fiscal management. Her business acumen and sympathetic response was praised in a letter from Benjamin when he detailed a severe financial setback. He had not told his wife about this problem, fearing her lack of strength and resourcefulness in a difficult situation, since she was a woman. One does wonder exactly how he viewed his sister Emily!

It becomes increasingly clear that family and friends flocked to her doorstep to receive more than financial advice. Emily had always been perceived as a feminine "Father Confessor" by the members of the Philadelphia network. Sallie Holley continued to remind her of the importance of this role even in their old age, "Thee always was kind of Father Confessor to folks" was her oft-repeated sentiment. In the 1870s Emily began to be perceived by her Sherwood neighbors in this same light. "Startled by a call while at breakfast, went and there stood L.S., sad and statue like, saying 'I have not a friend left.' I drew her in & heard the sad story." This empathetic response can be noted over and over again during these years. While nursing her cousin Phebe Wood she was given the main burden of responsibility by the other relatives, prompting her to comment "whenceforth I did not know unless it was that I was a kind of king log to steady them." Not infrequently poor black and white young women arrived at her home seeking work, food, lodging and education. In one entry, Emily pondered one such situation, "L.M. here. She seems to be another waif thrown on my shore. (Others) do not want her, so the question is what can be done with this girl. She is from N.C. and wants to go to school."

Emily found this new community role and her growing positive self-image an unexpected but welcome change. Thus when she failed to receive community support in matters she highly valued she noted her disappointment and felt rather angry. When she circulated a woman's suffrage petition it was taken as a joke and both male and female neighbors refused to seriously discuss the right of women to vote. When she brought in a radical agent from the Temperance Publishing House for a local meeting she "was rather coldly treated because I introduced him," although she added that she "thought his address convinced them there was no heresy about him." She was attempting to awaken the community's sense of concern over the reform issues of temperance, woman's rights and moral purity but feared that instead of arousing Sherwood's slumbering social conscience, she was becoming more apathetic like its inhabitants by burying her sense of duty under a mountain of purely social activities.

In a introspective mood, Emily reflected on her occasional relapses into an unhealthy physical and mental state and attributed them in part to the constant round of social events. The literary and debating club meetings however were not resented since at these Emily was able to join low-level intellectual discussions. She realized that these could not compare with the intellectual activities of the Philadelphia network yet felt satisfied that at least she was exchanging ideas on a regular basis. She admitted the importance these club meetings had in her life and acknowledged "always feel(ing) best when I have given out an idea" and "empty when I give no thot to anybody." The local sewing society, established to assist the county orphans asylum, on the other hand, was deemed a pleasant charitable exercise for some but certainly not for Emily. She disgustedly wished "she could walk away from all sewing societies forever" yet did not. Having accepted her new public role, she even remained active in the sewing society, fearing to set a poor example for apathetic Sherwoodians in any charitable area.

Her reaction to her new role and image at home was mixed. She did receive ego satisfaction, develop a better self-image, and manage to receive some intellectual stimulation; but Sherwood was neither Philadelphia nor Virginia. Her perspective of life during these years is best described with an incident that took place on nearby Lake Cayuga. On a day trip to Ithaca Emily observed a group of students on the boat traveling on the lake to town. Watching their activities closely, she commented in a revealing remark that "the pathos comes from all hearts near the surface of all gayety." This seemingly random comment so perfectly focuses on the way in which Emily saw the juxtaposition of joy and sorrow in her life and the lives of those around her. Happiness was to be captured for a brief, fleeting moment from the clutches of depression, unhappiness or despair. She viewed pathos as her enemy and wrote "if I could only conquer my gloom I should feel that the triumph more than paid for the inheritance. I want to beat my foe in open field." Only death could end this battle and at times it seemed to her that "the pleasantest thing in the gloom w'd be to crawl into my grave." The intervals between these moments lengthened however and Emily's reiteration of feelings of anguish and despair became almost non-existent after 1881.

As the second decade of America's Gilded Age progressed and Emily's depressions and inner struggles diminished, the rhythm of her life in Sherwood followed a smoother, quieter current. She had resigned herself to a dormant existence interrupted only with periodic visits to Philadelphia and the South. She saw herself change from an aggressive creature fighting in a hostile environment to a directionless "poor blind spinner in the sun." She poignantly pencilled "triste comme un libou" in her diary to describe her feelings as she patiently cared for her ailing father. She now affectionately referred to him as though he were a quiet, gentle child who sought her loving attention and nursing skills. She sat up with him while he was ill, at times impairing her own health to nurse him. She learned how to capture his wandering attention while she again painted his portrait and discussed their financial situation. The depressions, isolation, alienation and self-abnegation became part of the past, while a peaceful acceptance held sway over the present and eclipsed any thoughts of the future.

Abruptly in May 1881 this long-sought-after peace was shattered when Slocum suffered a cerebral stroke which left him partially paralyzed and deprived of speech. Emily, while nursing him did not find the time to write to her friends or to keep a daily record. Margaret Burleigh understood the deep relationship which existed between Emily and her father. She also recognized the unique place Slocum filled in Emily's life and tried to prepare Emily for his death, "My thoughts are continually turning to him and more esp. to thee— thinking how sad it must be to receive to thy tender questions no reply from the beloved voice which through all the years of thy life has never failed thee before."

Within six weeks Slocum Howland was dead. Margaret Burleigh again tried to comfort Emily who was "bending under a sense of desolation never before experience." Emily's loss was total "for hitherto whatever else might fail, dear father was always there." Emily was incapable of comforting herself with the traditional religious thought that Slocum had awakened to eternal joy in a life after death. "He was so used to this life and comfortable in it that it must be hard for him to have to leave it—a feeling I could not reason down that he was homesick there." Emily remained in their Sherwood home alone after Slocum's funeral although the Philadelphia network tried to convince her to leave "that desolated house." They attempted to impress upon Emily that she was, at last, free to live and travel with them. In June, 1881 however Emily Howland alone knew her unusual plans for life without her father.

8

To Seek a Clearer Vision

Ambivalence and indecisiveness had been Emily Howland's most frequent response to conflict and change at critical points in her life. With Slocum's death Emily now faced a complex situation which demanded that she make a number of important choices. By this point, it would be natural to expect Emily to shrink from this decision-making confrontation and to act with uncertainty by vacillating between alternative courses of action, as she had done so frequently in the past.

With her father's death Emily had received a substantial inheritance which included two county farms, Arcadia and the Sherwood homestead. In addition to the real estate she had received enough cash and stocks to make her a comfortably wealthy woman for the rest of her life. As she remarked after going over the accounts with her brother William: "What a heavy weight so much money seems." With no familial responsibilities, Emily was now free to pursue any life style she chose without fear of parental recrimination. William and Benjamin had always given her support when she strayed from the more traditional female roles and appear to have respected their sister's need for independence, intellectuality, and dominance.

These needs could best be satisfied in an environment of friends, intellectuals and reformers—in short, with the Philadelphia network. Yet as early as the 1850s Emily had questioned Margaret Burleigh about the severe disadvantages associated with the life of the female reformer-intellectual. This very important point bears directly upon Emily Howland's subsequent behavior and more particularly, upon her actions after Slocum's death. Emily had shown awareness of the great psychological cost paid by the female reformer in terms of community and familial ridicule, contempt or hostility. She perceived female reformers as threatening both family and community with their radical visions of social and cultural change. From her earliest contact with the Philadelphia group she had been sensitive to the conflicting images of her friends; they were hailed as saints and prophets from some quarters while receiving abuse and rejection from others. Her view of the feminist included the painful as well as the satisfying aspects of playing such a non-traditional role. The female reformer had "bleeding feet" as she walked along the unpopular path of social change. In an early letter to Burleigh, Emily saw her fellow female abolitionists as "walking thro fire" and felt that she had to ask if it would "not be wrong to waver" as she attempted to follow in her more radical sisters' footsteps.

Her long history of indecisiveness and ambivalence toward taking a more total activist's role, as had Grew, Holley, Anthony, Stanton, Stone and other prominent nineteenth century reformers, stemmed in part from a dual perception of the costs as well as the rewards of activist labor. From her earliest writings, Emily admitted that she was unable to face hostility, contempt, or ridicule. She needed to be dominant and independent but she also wished to be admired, respected and beloved. She needed more than the goodwill, respect and support of her Philadelphia network. As she grew older what Sherwoodians and her extended family thought of her actions and ideals occupied increasing amounts of space in her diary.

She clearly delineated her reasons for rejecting traditional female roles when she embraced various social reforms. Emily did not express however an equally clear delineation of her choice not to totally commit herself to the reformer's role. When she rejected motherhood and marriage she became an ideological feminist but failed to become an active crusader as other single feminists, notably Susan B. Anthony, had. When Emily rejected government policies in relation to freedmen she took the initial reformist steps with her purchase of Arcadia, but she failed to remain actively involved in the project and to keep up the momentum of change after the first six months. Although still intellectually committed to the education, and social and economic advancement of Southern blacks, Emily retreated from continuing in the role of active reformer. During her "cat in a strange garret" period she furnished both the black and national women's rights movement with money rather than with her time. To try to bring about change through these unpopular actions was to risk rejection and the accompanying psychological ego damage. To financially underwrite the radical activities of others was a far less alienating form of commitment.

With the close of the war and reconstruction work the nineteenth century female reformers lost many of the socially approved or accepted institutional bases from which they could put their ideological beliefs into practice. It would be another two decades before settlement houses began to move effectively into this breach, with Jane Addams best exemplifying the new socially approved female reformer. Emily's behavior and partial commitment to reform clearly represents one way in which a number of women at the time responded to the feminist movement and reform cause in general. They were, that is, simultaneously attracted by radical social ideologies yet repulsed by the dangers affiliation with the movements to advance these ideologies would entail. We hear of the Susan B. Anthonys, the Elizabeth Cady Stantons, and the Victoria Woodhulls who devoted their thinking and activity to reform without evidencing fear of censure or rejection. We also hear of the Catherine Beechers who assumed an active, independent personal role in defense of traditional domesticity, thus adjusting to their ambivalence on an intellectual level. Those whom we do not hear of are the countless women attracted to reform, perhaps active for short periods on a local level, who ultimately retreated to the safety of the family circle. Emily chose one of several options by which a woman could respond to the reform mentality of the mid-nineteenth century.

Emily Howland's type of commitment to reform may also be viewed as a bridge between Susan B. Anthony and Jane Addams in the evolution of women's role in American social reform. Anthony and early female reformers worked outside of the social system since such roles for females were neither recognized nor legitimate. By the time of Jane Addams and the early progressives the female reformer was no longer a social pariah, so that Emily's partial commitment to reform movements would be increasingly less valid. Emily's response was formed at a time when popular perceptions of these movements wère undergoing a critical change from examining women-as-reformers to a primary emphasis on ideological content first and sex distinctions second. Anthony came of age as this women-as-reformers syndrome reached its peak in the 1840s and 1850s. Emily's initial commitment had come a decade later when previously held preceptions of women in reform were in a state of flux, while the later history of Jane Addams meteoric rise and fall in public opinion attests to the increasing importance placed on the content of the reform rather than the woman.

Emily was perhaps incapable of changing her type of commitment to social reform but in 1881 she had the opportunity to alter the degree and intensity if she wished. She had the freedom, wealth, and familial independence to work totally for change in the status of women or blacks, for temperance, education or moral purity. But other alternatives beckoned her as well. No longer tied by those invisible bonds to her family in Sherwood she could reject any sense of responsibility and indulge in the personal pleasures of worldwide travel and formal education. Her choice however was to continue to live in Sherwood and to spend the remainder of her days alternately supporting reformist activities and pursuing personal pleasure.

Her rejection of a total commitment to the Philadelphia group and the related rejection of an overt activist life style can be understood in terms of her position on the continuum of reformist commitment but questions of personality may be involved as well. When Emily visited with fellow members for long periods of time their relationships deteriorated rapidly suggesting that Emily had great difficulty when geographically close sustaining good interpersonal relations with the network over time. If this were the case her return to the group would necessitate strongly affective face-to-face relationships if such a reunion were to be successful on a permanent basis. It is possible that Emily recognized and shrank from this situation as she had similarly retreated from other relationships which required a marked degree of warmth, giving, understanding and love. To write to her Philadelphia friends would satisfy her emotional needs without the strain of daily primary encounters. Also in view of her choice of only partial commitment to social change guilt and inadequacy were bound to spring up in Emily as she saw her fellow members dedicate their lives to temperance, women's suffrage, and moral purity. In Sherwood, via correspondence, this threat would be much diminished.

Emily decided to make a new life for herself free of these threats and compatible with her need for independence, responsibilities, autonomy and respect in her home community. As if to herald the start of this new life Emily began to remodel the old homestead, making major interior renovations and eventually adding a west wing that transformed the appearance of the house. She did not plan to live in this large house by herself and by early spring of 1882 the reasons for such alterations became understandable. When the community's Sherwood Select School outgrew its quarters in the house on the northeast corner of the crossroads south of Emily's home she decided to build a new high school on land she had donated next to her house. Realizing the growing need for higher education, she was offering high school training to many who otherwise would never have had the opportunity in a village so small and rural. A contemporary newspaper account called the finished elaborate rococo building "the finest structure of its kind outside the cities anywhere in New York State." When it opened in January, 1883 approximately sixty pupils filled the study hall and two recitation rooms. The three women teachers included Emily Howland's niece Isabel and the curriculum developed by Howland and the principal included Geography, Philosophy, Latin, French, Botany, Rhetoric, Astronomy, Physiology, History, Geometry, German, Physics, Chemistry and Higher Mathematics.

Many of these subjects reflect Emily's classical interests as well as her informal education and training over the last thirty years. A brochure of the Sherwood Select School stated that "the aim of this institution is the moral and intellectual development of pupils of both sexes. The government is entirely by moral suasion, pupils being taught, as far as possible to govern themselves."

Children from a distance boarded for the term in local homes; Emily's commodious house was used by the teachers who did not live within commuting distance. When the original principal retired seven years later Emily wrote in her diary that she had "built the school for Hepsibeth, and now she has retired and I have it on my hands." She had to manage the building, hire teachers and janitorial staff and support it since the small tuition fee of $10 per term did not adequately cover her expenses. This increasing responsibility matched Howland's growing interest and involvement in the direction of the school. Since the teachers and principals generally lived with her, she exerted a great influence on the choice of the curriculum and management. In 1907 the school was closed for a period of two years because its diploma did not admit graduates to all colleges. In 1909 after continuous and at times unpleasant debate with the Board of Regents of the state of New York, Emily reopened the school under their auspices. Since the community had rejected a proposal to fund a district public high school with taxes Howland offered to continue support for the school, paying all additional expenses above and beyond those paid by the state and through tuition fees. The property was placed in the hands of trustees and was to belong to the community as long as it was maintained as a school. Emily was determined that "the light must not go out in this community" and that the "gates of knowledge be kept open." By supporting universal education, Emily had found her place in the Sherwood community and had gained not only support but also respect and esteem. From 1909 until she turned the school over to the state to become part of a centralized public school district, Emily controlled many if not all aspects of the school. In securing teachers she exhibited great deliberation. In a statement which reflected upon her own formal education and the impact Susanna Marriott had on her life, Emily wrote to a prospective teacher, "We want not only the learning of schools but a fine character, I regard the teacher's personality and influence as important as the knowledge that she may impart. Not seldom all the spiritual uplift that a child receives comes thru the teacher."

The annual closing exercises were important community events, with the local residents filling the large study hall. One participant in these exercises recalled that when Emily Howland would arise to give her annual address "a hush fell over the audience, an evidence of the love and respect which everyone felt for her."

The children of Sherwood were not the only ones to receive financial aid for their education. When in 1868 Emily and Carrie Putnam were traveling by boat down Lake Cayuga on the first leg of their journey back to Northumberland County, they had entered into a conversation on coeducation at Cornell University with Ezra Cornell and a New York Tribune reporter. Their talk had ended with Cornell's suggestion, perhaps partly in jest, that if Howland would find and support women interested in attending Cornell he would not oppose their admission. Emily took this conversation seriously and from the 1870s until her death gave interest-free loans and gifts to female friends, family and neighbors to attend Cornell.

The community became increasingly indebted to her for the education of their sons and daughters. It was a debt however Emily seemed to enjoy, and she would frequently respond to those she had helped, "thee need not repay me, pass it on to someone else."

After her father's death, Emily began to perceive her wealth as a public trust and the administration of it, in terms of community affairs, an important responsibility. In Sherwood alone she had given the building, property and $37,000 of her money in a little over forty years. She also gave thousands of dollars to over thirty Southern, technical, normal and industrial schools during these same forty years.

Throughout those years when Emily had lived in Sherwood with her father her interest in black education had never faltered. She continued to support the Howland School in Heathsville and contributed yearly donations to schools run by fellow network members Carrie Putnam, Sallie Holley and Cornelia Hancock. She sent books, building equipment, tuition and money to predominantly Southern black elementary and secondary schools before her father's death as different needs were brought to her attention. With Slocum's death, Emily was then free to contribute without parental consent and she exerted her new-found fiscal authority without hesitation. By 1890 the number of requests from newly established Southern black teaching and vocational schools increased so rapidly that, at times, a week without an appeal for funding was highly unusual. She often remarked to her friends in Sherwood that "the negro opened the book of life to me" when referring to her experiences during the war and reconstruction. With her return to Sherwood, Howland concentrated on funding black education so that a portion of the previously all white world would in turn be open to the blacks.

The 1890s marked the beginning of the yearly visits to Howland by the black educators in the Southern schools she supported. They explained their goals, the use of her money and provided an updating of the situation in their institutions. Emily felt that by meeting and corresponding with Booker T. Washington, Laurence Jones, Oswald Villard and William E. Dubois she was playing a critical role in the continuing struggle for black equality. In this manner she could work effectively for reform without alienating her community. Of perhaps greater psychological importance Emily herself, the Friends and other residents of Sherwood now were beginning to share a set of similar perceptions regarding this generous benefactor in their midst. For the first time, Emily's self-image was not in such drastic conflict with the public image of her held by the community; she now saw herself and was perceived as being active and satisfied in her chosen ministry in life—education.

As the century drew to a close, Emily exhibited interest in funding northern and western white schools including ones in Kansas, Idaho and the George Junior Republic in Freeville, New York. The thrust of these donations was often aimed in the direction of facilities and expanded education for females. Not surprisingly the majority of scholarships and loans which she gave yearly were awarded to young black and white women.

Emily felt that the apex of her satisfaction and sense of reward in relation to education was reached in the winter of 1913 during her "triumphal tour of the Southern schools," to which she had been a long and faithful benefactor. A prized snapshot of Emily shows her enthroned under a flower-decked canopy, crowned with roses, surrounded by young smiling black children. Emily felt that this was a rare testimonial to receive during her lifetime and interpreted it as a sign of respect and love from the people she had helped. From the point of view of today's mid-twentieth century changing view of race relations this portrait in paternalism may be viewed with a mixture of cynicism, condescension and embarrassed incredulity. When placed in the context of late nineteenth and early twentieth century benevolence however it is possible to read both Emily's perceptions and behavior and the blacks' actions and responses in a far different light.

Her generosity and relations with black educators such as Washington may have been tinged with paternalism and condescension but nevertheless were courageous acts to make at a time when the Southern blacks' social equality and civil rights were daily denied. Jim Crow laws, judicial and economic exploitation and lynching were facts of Southern life while more subtle, yet equally insidious, discriminatory Northern practices continued to keep blacks in a decidely inferior position within American society.

Emily Howland during her triumphal tour of the Southern schools in 1913.
(Courtesy Friends Historical Library of Swarthmore College)

Throughout those decades when race relations were deteriorating
to this point Emily Howland continued to entertain, support and
work with blacks, disregarding those all-pervasive rules for communicating with those of a different race. When Sojourner Truth was
on a speaking tour of western New York in 1878 Emily invited her to
stay at her home for four days. Although Emily from her upper-middle class white perspective felt Sojourner to be at times rather coarse
and vulgar, she nevertheless recognized Sojourner to be a "good and
wisely person," and considered her a "witty & original" friend.

Emily's vision, shared by a minority of white Americans at the turn
of the century, was that the ignorance of the Negro and the

problems caused by it "is the weakest link in the chain of American strength." Her educational work in Washington, contraband camps and Arcadia as well as her later funding projects, can all be viewed as attempts to forge better links in this chain. Emily consistently believed in the value of education for minorities and felt that both races gained by such actions.

Whether the black educators and children on Emily's triumphal tour viewed her with mock respect or sincere appreciation in her role of wealthy patron can only be a point of conjecture. Booker T. Washington's feigned subservience and role acting in the presence of white contributors to Tuskegee Institute has been recently suggested but the question of black response to white philanthropy will have to remain unanwered here. Her actions in supporting black education on the other hand, can be considered both humanitarian and deviant since it stemmed from her socially unacceptable humanist belief in the right to equality of opportunity for black persons within the United States.

If equality of opportunity best exemplified her values in relation to blacks, full equality with no equivocation best describes her attitude toward the role of women. Dating from her first public political statement on women's rights in 1844, Emily's feminist beliefs rarely wavered. A radical ideology based on women's rights to political, social and economic equality motivated Emily at various times during her long life even though it never was expressed in terms of an active national leadership role within a political organization. She was a member and the president of the Cayuga County Political Equality Club for many years and did much work on the grass roots level. Circulating petitions, arranging lectures and political meetings, writing legislators, attending state and national conventions and distributing literature and the *Woman's Journal* filled her days more fully after Slocum died. She had participated in some of these activities before his death when not incapacitated by severe depression. Emily's contribution to the nineteenth century woman's movement did not arise however out of her participation in the local and county women's suffrage campaigns. Instead, through her interest in education, her writing, her philanthropy and her relations with leading feminists, Emily performed a unique and valuable service to the women's movement.

Emily's organizational position during the 1870s and 1880s when the women's movement split between the conservative American and the more radical National Woman Suffrage Associations was far from clear. Her affiliation through the county organization was with Anthony's and Stanton's National which regarded women's rights as a broad cause encompassing more concerns than suffrage. The American group under Stone and Howe rested on the opposing social viewpoint which stressed state work and community approval and support for the franchise almost exclusively. Emily subscribed to the American's *Woman's Journal,* distributing it to members of her family and community and frequently giving yearly gift subscriptions to many acquaintances.

Emily was attracted to both organizations; the National wholeheartedly advocated, in an aggressive and unorthodox manner, a cause in which Emily believed. It was also run by two women whom she knew and respected. Her friendship with Stanton dated back to the early 1850s when Emily helped the Cayuga County feminists implement Stanton's state legislative proposals on behalf of widows. Emily met Susan B. Anthony later in the fifties and did not draw as close to her as she did to Stanton in the early years of their friendship. Only in the eighties as Howland emerged from her depressions and into her new life did her relationship with Anthony deepen and grow. As Stanton became involved in the divorce question and the educated franchise, Emily began to feel a growing compatibility with the increasingly less militant Susan B. Anthony. Anthony's indefatigable energy and willingness to speak at even the smallest gatherings such as the Sherwood Strawberry Festival endeared her to Emily. Moreover, Anthony's interest in the plight of all women coincided with Emily's broad egalitarian interpretation of the woman's movement. When the Cayuga County Political Equality Club tried to sponsor a women's educational and industrial union in Auburn for all classes and nationalities of women, Anthony's concern and Emily's grass root support helped make it a reality. By the mid-1890s, these two long-time, yet very different, advocates of women's rights were calling one another "Aunt Susan" and "Aunt Emily."

The Philadelphia group on the other hand, under the considerable influence of Mary Grew, chose in 1871 to align themselves with the American Woman Suffrage Association. Emily's position proved to be that of a bridge between members of both

Susan B. Anthony (seated) and Emily Howland in the study of Emily's home in Sherwood, New York. (Courtesy Friends Historical Library of Swarthmore College)

groups. Her New York affiliation was with Anthony and Stanton yet she could well understand the appeal of the American group to her Philadelphia friends. The mantle of prestige and respectability placed on the American group by its leader, Julia Ward Howe, would certainly have looked attractive to Emily in light of her reluctance to act militantly. Similarly, their singlemindedness in pursuing the franchise by avoiding related side issues would again be compatible with her need for sharp technical focus. Furthermore, the American Association hoped to manipulate and gain community interest and support by avoiding volatile moral issues in their pursuit of woman suffrage. Howland again would be comfortable with this strategy; for in carrying out such a campaign in the county and Sherwood community she could work for reform with less fear of alienating friends, relatives and neighbors. This consideration perhaps was most influential in her decision to support and distribute the *Journal* for so many years. That the differences between the two organizations could be bridged successfully in the late '80s shows that Emily's position as fence-sitter between the two camps was ideologically possible, and became recognized when Alice Stone Blackwell worked to merge these two groups in 1890.

Although Emily's peripheral political role and political activities seem of greatest interest to the historian, other aspects of her feminist activities and beliefs are actually of even more interest and significance. Emily's home named "Tanglewild" after Slocum's death became one of several centers for rest, relaxation, intellectual conversation and reformist action planning for county, New York and national women's movement members. Anthony, Anna Howard Shaw, Elizabeth Smith Miller, Eliza Wright Osborne, Dr. Amanda Sanford Hickey, Ida H. Harper and Harriet May Mills were some of the better known leaders who accepted Emily's hospitality and used her home as an informal station in their state and national organizatonal networks. Women with facilities such as Emily Howland's existed throughout the country and provided leaders with meager incomes, as was the case with Shaw and Anthony, with a temporary home, rest and the emotional support of sisterhood. The Reverend Shaw reminisced in her autobiography of the informal network in Cayuga County, New York which had come into existence in the closing years of the nineteenth century. In the years between Slocum's death and the dawn of the new century, Emily slowly became incorporated into a circle of women who were feminists, reformers, professional working women and in some cases, intellectuals. The main function of this network in contrast with the Philadelphia group was to provide a respite from reformist activities within a supportive sisterhood based on similar belief and value systems—a turn of the century consciousness-raising group. As Shaw wrote "the best talk I have heard anywhere was that to which I used to listen in the home of Mrs. Eliza Wright Osborne in Auburn, New York when Mrs. Stanton, Susan B. Anthony, Emily Howland, Elizabeth Smith Miller, Ida Hasted Harper, Miss Mills and I gathered there for our occasional weekend visits. Many human and feminine touches brightened the lofty discussions that were constantly going on and the varied characteristics of our leaders cropped up in amusing fashion."

Emily looked forward to state and national women's rights conventions and occasionally spoke at these. She attended an international women's rights convention in London in 1903 and was thrilled to join the group having tea with Queen Victoria. These organizational activities, however, belie the depth of her commitment to the struggle for women's equal rights. Her writings more than these activities or friendships can be viewed as her most important legacy to the movement; her words blaze across the pages of her diary and correspondence as she recorded anger, frustration, and joy in the progress toward the goal of equal rights.

The evolution of her feminist ideology was logically, precisely and thoroughly presented in her writings over a sixty year span. She fought against equating women with "home graces," arguing that the house was equally man's sphere. She scoffed at the idea of the possible loss of feminine qualities, feeling that this was a sugar-coated pill given to women by men, based on flattery, to further the continuation of "their imagined superiority." What most aroused her ire were attacks on women's inequality of mental powers "as for (this), there has been no fair trial to test this, but so far as the intellect of woman has been permitted cultivation, it has proved itself not inferior." Implicit in her cultural rather than genetic argument was an overriding humanistic belief which she considered the logical conclusion of feminist ideas. "Women are human beings . . . they need human rights. Whatever rights or duties men have discovered to be needful for their well-being as members of the human family are equally a necessity for woman's well-being and doing."

From a more pragmatic point of view, Emily was angered by a paradoxical situation she faced in 1891 when becoming the first female bank director in the state of New York. She was unable to vote yet was granted increased fiscal authority and taxation. "Have we a representative gov't when one half of the people have no voice in it?" she asked the Suffrage Committee of the Constitutional Convention in the Assembly Chamber at Albany on June 7, 1894. She threw the old axiom at them that "taxation without representation is tyranny" (and continued to reiterate this to every tax collector and government agent until she had the chance to cast her first ballot three decades later). To the august committee she closed her speech with a courageous if somewhat abusive statement by quoting the rather unpoetic lines of a popular doggeral: "Go put your creed into your deed nor longer speak with double tongue."

Emily felt that she was living in a transition period in the world of woman's work, where her service to the world was in a constant state of change. "Our opportunity is the measure of our responsibility" she wrote in expressing her resentment of the childlike position of women who were forced to live as "perpetual minors, controlled absolutely" by men. In expressing this injustice to women she attempted to place it in a broader humanist perspective in a letter to the local newspaper editor which ended with

Laboring man and laboring woman
Have one glory and one shame,
Everything that's done inhuman
Injures both alike the same.

In her view woman's opportunities extended beyond the narrow confines of suffrage, for their duties and responsibilities uniquely influenced the human family. Women were ideally suited to effect change since they could step into the vacuum created by man's estrangement from humanist concerns. In other words Emily was advocating that women take over the reins of moral power. She fully subscribed to the Emersonian phrase "civilization is the power of good women." She praised the WCTU, the largest organization of women in the world, for its comprehensive benevolent aims of "strengthening the weak and undoing the heavy burden of wrong." She saw a need "for the moral elevation of the surrounding community" and attempted to gather neighboring women together to work toward this goal. She held weekly parlor meetings in her crusade for moral purity and each summer hosted a lawn meeting with an attendance of over one hundred to discuss efforts and the crusade for the next year.

In 1883 Emily had mused over her new life in Sherwood and had in turn made a pledge which was to guide her actions for the rest of the century, "I see clearly that I must return to active work for humanity. I need it, the work needs me. I am wasting & growing odious at mere housework." She found the work, in part, in a community crusade for moral purity. Men were "tearing down what civilization has striven to build up—pure living and high thinking," Emily commented to her niece at this time. She had imbibed the words of "our sainted Frances Willard" and the crusading spirit of this age so thoroughly that she was soon advocating that "the Bible & Shakespeare & Faust, all (be) refined to suit what we require of our associates & of our reading, the degree of purity in thought & speech wh. is the ideal in this age."

Emily expected those around her to spend their lives and energy striving to attain this ideal. When one of the young Arcadians whom Emily had educated in her home, at Union Springs and later at Howard University, became involved with a married man in Virginia Emily's reaction was one of disbelief, bewilderment, hurt, anger and finally a despairing, but gentle forgiveness. She asked her never to marry, perhaps viewing this as an apt punishment for what she referred to, in her correspondence, as the young woman's "crime." Emily alternately viewed the woman as a "sinner," a "wounded bud" or "one coming from the depths of sin" who must be reeducated to walk again on the path of virtue.

Emily was nativistic, as were many of her upper-class nineteenth century American feminist sisters, and not above such references to the Irish as "one century removed from the bog." Yet Emily's moral concern overrode her cultural bias so that she became directly concerned with the fate of her "fallen sisters," no matter what class, ancestry or race. She found homes in the country for such black and immigrant young women, usually referring to them as her protégées. Here they would be given the necessary care, protection and education to repent their sinful past and join the crusade for morality. Emily received requests from all over the country and from India to sponsor educational and vocational programs for "fallen" or distressed women. She saw herself as part of an active national and international sisterhood based on the search for moral purity. As one correspondent noted, "My soul goes out to you as an *honorable* woman—Alas! I have reason to dread affiliation with the morally unsound!"

By the close of the century Emily was spending increasingly large portions of her day dispensing money to different reforms but she was also beginning to use her inheritance on more pleasurable, less altruistic pursuits. In 1885 she took her first extended vacation, a three month Mediterranean trip where she sketched, read, wrote and visited the countryside as well as the cities in Greece and Italy. By 1900 Howland had visited Europe, North Africa, Mexico, California and the Caribbean, leaving home for months and on one occasion for two years without excessive guilt feelings. On these essentially educational and social trips Emily insisted on excellent accommodations as she toured with different groups of wealthy independent upper-class matrons and spinsters who had both the time and money to travel from country to country without a rigid schedule. She took courses, attended lectures, seminars, painted and sketched, read and visited museums and cathedrals. At times, Emily would take off on side trips alone tarrying to paint or sketch national monuments, rejoining the ever-changing groups when she pleased. William and Hannah at home in Sherwood handled her business affairs while the Sherwood Select School was managed by the principal living at Tanglewild. Emily thoroughly enjoyed these pleasant interludes and returned from most vacations with a remark about assuming "those cares which certainly are waiting" once again. She continued her winter trips to Philadelphia, Virginia and South Carolina, missing them only when on an extended tour elsewhere.

In an interview with a reporter Emily once commented upon the beneficial effect of these welcome interruptions and startled him with a related thought. "I wish there were compulsive education for women over seventy. Every woman has something she has always wanted to do and couldn't because there wasn't time enough. When we reach the Isle of Leisure, past 70, that is our opportunity. Since there is no such thing as a School for the Aged, we must make our own school. We can teach ourselves." After her seventieth birthday Emily's various trips had been an effective School for the Aged for her. In addition to traveling Emily had also embarked on a variety of different projects, intellectual endeavors and activities never attempted before she turned seventy. Her days were no longer filled with household drudgery but occupied by living her new philosophy of "self help by helping others." She enjoyed having young children and the Sherwood Select School teachers in her home. Entertaining and informal discussions of international events rounded out her late evening hours. "I do not like to dwell on my own past, it is depressing," she wrote Carrie Putnam. "Like my father I must go forward to keep up cheer."

Emily continued to reveal her more personal thoughts and opinions to those in the Philadelphia network. As old age reduced their mobility and the number of activities, the correspondence between the members seemed to take on increased importance for them. The Carrie Putnam-Emily Howland correspondence typifies the changing function of their communication, for they became even more affectionate, dependent, empathetic and revealing as they reached Emily's Isle of Leisure. "Since your inspiring letters come no more, I find a something gone out of my life" Emily wrote after a brief interruption in the flow of their letters. As death reduced the number in the group, those remaining drew even closer together although separated for large portions of time each year. Emily would note in her diary following news of the death of one of these friends her fear that soon there would be "no contemporary who knew what I knew" left. Grew, Burleigh, Holley, Reed, Jones, and Robinson all died before the new century began.

Death, a constant companion of the Philadelphia network, also visited among Emily's newer New York friendship group. As Stanton, Wright, Anthony, Bradley, Sanford, and Osborne died during the last years of the nineteenth and the beginning ones of the twentieth century Emily confided in her oldest and most faithful friend, her diary, about "How poor the world had grown of late."

Benjamin, Emily's younger brother, had died in an accident at his mill in the Catskills the year after Slocum's death. Emily's grief had been severe for between her and Benjamin there existed a loving, if somewhat distant, bond. When Hannah died in 1902 after a long illness in which she suffered greatly Emily lost her closest friend and "sister." Her grief was tempered with relief, knowing that Hannah's death was a release from the unbearable pain she had endured for the last few years. Emily's brother William died less than two years later and Emily could not contain her sorrow for his death as well as for the deaths of these other close friends and relatives. "The world looks dark tonight, the shadow of the woes of the world is over me," she told her diary in response to the deaths surrounding her. "I thought of the loved and gone and wondered if they knew & saw & enjoyed as they did in life. Sometimes the feeling of being alone is depressing. My contemporary relatives & nearly all my friends (are) on the other side."

Emily did not succumb to depression as she had during both puberty and menopause. At times, she felt searing loneliness but she had grown accustomed to a high degree of loneliness due to her emotional distance and geographic separation from her closest contemporaries during different stages of her life.

She was determined to make the best possible use out of the last years of her life. As she told Carrie Putnam, "I believe we have more to make us glad than sad, that life has given us of its best in the way of health, opportunity and friends, and however far from our ideal in achievement or in the spiritual life we may feel that we have meant well to humanity and have been generous seekers to the end."

When Emily reached the "Isle of Leisure" she managed to maintain a faith in the beauty of human nature. More important, she had gained a sense of "hopefulness" in which the giving of self was an integral ingredient. Her self-image finally coincided with her highly positive public image. As old age approached, Emily viewed herself in a less harsh and demanding light and saw to her surprise an individual who had dedicated a good share of her life to educating, improving and serving humanity. She looked at her achievements and was satisfied with the way she had handled the money, trust and responsibility placed in her hands after her father's death. Finally, she was humble, but secretly pleased, by her substantial intellectual progress in the past twenty years and her recognition by others as "a woman of advanced thought" who kept "pace with education." In short, Emily, the Sherwood community and the remainder of the New York and Philadelphia groups all viewed Emily Howland as a doer and seeker, as an intellectual and a reformer, and as a humanitarian. Emily, at last, was at peace with herself. She posed the question in her diary whether her life now was ready to end. "The last time I saw Lucretia Mott she said of herself, 'it is time to be gone.' Is it true of me?" But it was not time for Emily to be gone for her work, struggle, joys and sorrows were not to end before she could address herself to the intellectual and reformist challenges of the early twentieth century.

9

The Final Odyssey

> The streets were well beflagged every house had a flag out, plenty of stupid & speckled patriotism or exultation over the war that is on us.—(From Emily Howland's diary April 11, 1917)

Emily Howland, age eighty-nine, had lived through the "great war" between the states and later had lectured and written tracts against United States imperialism and aggression in the Philippines and Central America. Now, four days after the United States had officially entered the first global war, Emily could only write her caustic words helplessly in her journal. Her speeches, essays and letters advocating peace between nations and men had been ineffectual, as had those of far more active pacifists. As the pace of living in the early twentieth century accelerated, her means of communicating her beliefs and values rested more and more in the written word. Her letters to state and national legislators, to international diplomats and to pacifist groups expressed her fear of the consequences of war on the nations and the people of the world. In contrast with her more militant feelings during the Civil War, Emily now felt that "hatreds only begat more hatreds and violence more & worse violence. We must think peace, talk peace, work for peace, educate for peace."

Dating from United States' involvement in the Philippines in 1899, she had dedicated substantial amounts of energy and time to criticizing imperialism and global militarism, while advocating the humanitarian benefits of a pacifist world view. When preparedness parades were enthusiastically advanced throughout the Northeast in 1916 and criticism of national pacifist leaders such as Jane Addams mounted, Emily realized that her idealistic view of international and interpersonal relations were held by a small, and almost universally scorned, minority. She was grieved and alarmed by the hatreds and violence but felt helpless to effect change. She believed that each human life was sacred, that each woman and man was a child of God, and that love expressed through creative action, was the only power that could overcome hatred, prejudice and fear. God lived in every man and woman, Emily maintained; it was therefore a short step for her to take when she denied the right of the state to set arbitrary and artificial barriers to the humanitarian instinct of each person. Just as she had refused to let the government determine her position on slavery, so now, over half a century later, she denied the government's right to tell her who the enemy was. She refused to believe the atrocity stories circulating about the Germans and cautioned those around her to examine and analyze such propaganda. The Quaker way of believing and acting would be to speak directly to each person's humanitarian instinct through non-violent acts in the hope of putting the violent individual into contact with the Inner Light which Quakers believe exists in every person. Emily Howland's speeches and essays on peace rest entirely on this Quaker base with one important difference; "War has been the greatest foe of woman. Is not this the work that should start a second Crusade of the women of our land, to girdle the globe with the message of peace, as the only principle by which nations can live, by which human existence can continue?"

She had grown to hold strongly humanistic beliefs which increasingly transcended her feminism after she passed the age of seventy; yet she was very much a woman of her times. She, as so many leading feminists in the early twentieth century, continued to view woman as a morally and ethically superior being ideally suited for humanitarian work. Her humanism, in contrast, was directly interconnected with her increasing compatibility with the faith and practices of the Religious Society of Friends. She began to subscribe to *The Friend* again, read tracts of Quaker actions and beliefs and spent long hours discussing twentieth century Quakerism with a dear young friend and Quaker minister and teacher, Agnes Tierney.

As one chronicler of the twentieth century Quaker peace movement wrote: "The Quakers do not believe that the Kingdom of God is at hand, or even in sight, but they are resolved to live and act as if the Kingdom had already come, on grounds that if no one does, then the Kingdom will never come." Emily began to embrace this Quaker thought and action as she took a more comfortable position within the Society once again. Her return to Quakerism can be traced to the active participation of early twentieth century Quakers in social concerns. She received no satisfaction or fulfillment from purely theological discussions or philosophical lectures on theological themes for they only "inclined my mind to wander just as it did under the infliction of long mtgs in childhood & grew as tired as then." When she reminisced on her attraction to the Unitarian Church for its blend of the metaphysical and practical work, she found that this same combination had been evident in Quakerism. Now, however, she was ready to embrace it, realizing that it spoke directly to her growing need to integrate her social concerns with spiritual reflection.

Clearly Emily's renewed relationship with Quaker practices and beliefs can be viewed in yet another light as well. She wrote once that "a purposeless life is the most dreary one in the world." As the second decade of the twentieth century began to draw to a close, she realized the limitations advancing old age had placed upon her. She had to restrict her activism to writing and occasional speeches. She could no longer move around with the physical freedom of her youth and middle age. She was becoming lame, easily tired and her sore, painful knees were a continual problem to her. Her hearing was failing which, at times, proved a mixed blessing. This deteriorating physical condition made visiting and social activities increasingly difficult and the hours for reflection and reformist writing longer. Even if her physical health were that of a younger woman she would have found few contemporaries to communicate and visit with. Carrie Putnam, who had understood and loved Emily perhaps more than any other member of the Philadelphia network had died in December of 1916. Their correspondence during the last years of Carrie Putnam's life stands as a beautiful and moving tribute to these two women's friendship. Calling one another "auld lang syne," these women took decidedly different paths to coping with aging and death. Carrie, although aware of women's suffrage and peace reform, retreated more and more into the past where she had witnessed so many historic events and lived such a useful, purposeful life. Emily, ever determined "to strive to overcome weakness & failure," challenged both the present and future by acting on the social concerns of today which would most influence tomorrow. A return to the Society of Friends enabled Emily to accomplish the task of leading a purposeful life more efficiently. Her return to the Friends was not essentially a step back to relive or renew her ties with the past but rather another lineal step forward in her struggle for growth which would only be stopped by death.

Emily Howland and her good friend abolitionist Caroline F. (Carrie) Putnam circa 1915. (Courtesy Friends Historical Library of Swarthmore College)

With Carrie Putnam's death she had lost all in her Philadelphia network except Cornelia Hancock. The New York network fared no better and Emily resigned herself to a life to be lived without contemporary or near-contemporary friends and relatives. Those who knew her during these years compare her emotional state to the "Rock of Gibralter": steady, content, placid, serene, deeply conscientious and spiritual yet full of warmth, humor and common sense.

The warmth, humor and common sense make frequent appearances in diaries, but the stable emotional state described by those who lived with her points to a discrepancy between the diaries, or more correctly, her inner life and feelings and her public image. She had always used her diary as confidant but obviously the need increased as those persons closest to her died. She wrote of the frustrations of working for peace, with the Sherwood Select School's management and direction, with women suffrage campaigns, and with old age. She also began to reestablish and strengthen the bonds with the dead members of the Philadelphia and New York networks by annually rereading and editing their correspondence with her. A few days each year, usually in the midst of winter, Emily would immerse herself in the past and relive the events and emotions of another century. At these times, she would delete or destroy some of the material but rarely gave reasons for this self-editing.

This editing was one of several ways in which this woman prepared for her death and the perpetuation of her memory after death. She realized late in life the value of her diaries, although she continued to reiterate frequently that her words were not meant "for the public eye." Her editing actions nevertheless belie these statements. She also acknowledged the value of recording her memories of many national reform leaders. In some of her correspondence with Alice Stone Blackwell during the 1920s, Emily examined the past in the hope of clarifying events and relationships between suffrage leaders for posterity.

When she had finished this task of editing she would then return to the concerns of the present and the future, leaving these dear friends and the memory of their relationships for another year. Immersing herself in the past proved to be a yearly catharsis for her. She gained emotional satisfaction in this brief looking-backwards and then turned a serene face towards the younger, non-contemporary friends and relatives in her midst. In this manner, she was following her own advice from a earlier time: "As I see friend after friend depart, life grows more desolate, I realize that work only can make the voids endurable, live away from self."

Perhaps Emily downplayed the negative affective aspects of her personality, giving the impression of stoicism to those around her, by spending her day writing for reforms, and on the management of the Sherwood Select School. Such a schedule left little time and energy for developing a full affective psychological life. Her yearly contact with friends and relatives was one of two ways she selected to channel the direction and intensity of her emotional life. Rereading

old correspondence and reliving past experiences certainly involved
the expression and interplay of complex emotions as would her daily
practice of writing her innermost thoughts, conflicts and feelings in
her diary. In these two ways she was able to achieve an outward
serenity by "living away from self" publicly and by filling the "unendurable voids" privately in her writing and reading.

When New York enfranchised women and later with the passage
of the Nineteenth Amendment, Emily could not celebrate this victory with the women with whom she had worked for so long in the
past. She was treated with deference as the last of the oldest generation of women's rights workers and was honored in the New York
suffrage victory parades but the beauty and the joy of the moment
was marred by the loneliness of her position. This was one of the rare
times in the twentieth century that she did not use wit as a weapon
against her increasingly isolated status.

As she grew older letters for donations for educational purposes
increased so quickly that she could not help but laugh at the obvious
connection between the increased begging and her old age. "Over-
whelmed am I with begging letters. There seems a fresh outburst.
Perhaps they think that I am so old that I will soon be beyond their
reach & they must all pitch on me now like vultures."

She accepted the daily problems which accompanied old age into
her life. In the middle of summer, she would light a fire on the
hearth "to keep peace with my old joints." Daily naps became an
accepted part of her routine as did sunning herself in her meticu-
lously kept garden. At least one hour each morning was spent dressing so that her days seemed even shorter than before. Around her
ninetieth birthday, she questioned the wisdom of setting specific
tasks of reading and writing for herself each day. Yet she continued
her traditional pattern of work and reading, feeling that "old age is
not a reprieve from anything that I can do." Emily had always demanded efforts and results from herself and her work far beyond the
more modest expectations of those around her. Now in her ninth
decade of living she continued to keep her demands of self at a high
level. She had been called upon to be the first woman bank director
in the United States when she joined the Board of Directors of the
Aurora National Bank in 1891. Now in her nineties she continued to
attend board meetings, to handle all her investments and to oversee
her farms. Her financial acumen had not failed her in old age and

the wisdom of her dealings is evident when reviewing the probate of her will; in October, 1929 her estate was in excess of one quarter of a million dollars.

Her greatest difficult with adjusting to aging was her increasing loss of agility and motor activities. She could do nothing quickly. Surprisingly she did not despair over her image as someone "unusual & in a way a curiosity in that I have tarried so long." She slowly grew used to the loneliness of being surrounded by people but "unable to hear & only occasionally being talked to." Her depiction of her life in a busy school-oriented household points to the increased invisibility of the aged as their sense of hearing and thus communication fades. An integral member, if not the token matriarchal head, of the Sherwood household, Emily paradoxically stood isolated in the calm center of the activity swirling around her.

Realizing that all her ties with Northumberland were broken with Carrie's death, Emily had turned her school over to the public school system of the state of Virginia and had disposed of the last of the land and the buildings with sadness and regret in 1921. "So I have no longer any thing in the place I have so long cherished," she painfully confessed in her diary.

She realized that the same provisions for the Sherwood Select School should be made with the state of New York school commission but found that decision far more difficult to put into action. Her daily life in the past few years had revolved around the school routine, semesters, and vacations. Management, teachers, courses and maintenance occupied many of her hours, filled the household and gave her life structure. Once the Sherwood Select School was incorporated into the public school system, her life would take a radical turn, isolating her still further from the community, friends and purposeful activity.

As a student and former principal of the Sherwood Select School recalled: "The school was a great unifying force in the community." The four day closing exercises held annually between 1913 and 1926 provided past and present residents of the Sherwood area with the opportunity to be reunited with former classmates, friends and family, if only for a brief time each year. And in the center of all this stood Emily. Her management and interest in the school was recognized and appreciated by those most closely associated with her and the school but all additionally recognized the need to change the status of the school from private to public. Expenses had increased, the state aid remained insignificant, and both Emily and her niece, Isabel, were supplementing the finances so that by 1925, Emily alone contributed $4,000. After her 95th birthday, she acknowledged that the twin problems of her advancing years and the heavy financial burden made her management of the school impossible. She turned to the New York Board of Regents in the hope of making Sherwood a public school, thereby insuring continuance of education for the Sherwood adolescents.

Thus, in early 1925, Emily soon found herself in an ironic, if not difficult, position. The community had to be informed of the procedure of establishing a public school system supported by state aid and taxes. As public meetings to discuss the proposal were held throughout the spring and early summer, she found that advocating centralization under the public school system faced strong and vocal opposition. She was now in the position of defending a proposal which if placed into effect would eradicate the most central force in her daily life and sever her strongest link to the community. Yet, she continued on this course, which was, in effect, one more form of preparing for her death. She agreed to give the buildings, grounds, $4,000 toward repairs and an additional endowment of $8,000. A tentative budget, centralization plan and tax schedule were drawn up, advertised and then voted on in Sherwood by the residents of the six neighboring districts on January 9, 1926. Her diary reflects her concern and relief that this issue which had dominated the community and her life over the past year was to be resolved at last. "All over thought has been on the Sherwood Select School mtg this afternoon. It was a momentous time. The fate of the school was to be decided. We found the place crowded outside with autos, inside with people, more men than women. 133 votes were cast. 105 for the continuance of the school, and 28 against it. I was called upon to speak, which I did from my heart."

Emily was then elected to the board of education but her duties and responsibilities from this point on would be insignificant when contrasted with the burden carried when the Sherwood Select School was a private school. When she signed the diplomas for the last time in June, 1926, she at long last expressed the pain and loss she felt. After ninety-eight years, however, she had evolved a healthful perspective, placing this experience in the context of events deeply felt throughout her long lifetime. Reflecting upon her longevity, she sensibly admitted that "there is a measure of sorrow in doing anything for the last time, that has been the order for years."

Her lameness, increasing lack of mobility, failing eyesight and deafness almost daily placed new limitations upon her. She had approved and rapidly adjusted to the vast technological changes taking place during the early twentieth century. She especially enjoyed the automobile, frequently marvelling at the new perspective this means of transportation placed upon her concepts of time, distance and speed. Daily motor trips around the county, usually chauffered by her neighbor, Samuel Bowen, pleased her immensely and served two important functions in her later years. On these rides, she could continue to return to the places of her youth—something which, considering her age and physical condition, would previously not have been possible. In addition, these rides gave her the opportunity of leaving Tanglewild, if only briefly. Emily had always had a definite dislike of feeling "shut-in" as she referred to it, since it reminded her painfully of the tightly controlled, restricted environment of her childhood. On these daily trips, she could go back in time and relive the experiences of former days or could view the changes in housing, population and agricultural technology taking place at rapid strides throughout the area. The auto also allowed her to visit relatives and Cornelia Hancock at Little Deer Island, Maine, and to take water cures at New York sanitariums.

The automobile was not the only invention Emily used extensively. Teachers who lived with her during the early 1920s recall with enthusiasm the story of Emily and the advent of the radio at Tanglewild.

> When I was a member of Miss Emily's household, radio sets with loud-speakers were just coming into popularity. Some of us were eager to have a set but our purses were too slim. Our sole hope seemed to be to persuade Miss Emily that she, even with dulled hearing, could find pleasure and stimulation in radio, but we were none too confident of success. A radio was brought out 'on trial' from Auburn, and the stage was set for the test. All available stations were cautiously sampled with volume low for we had to be sure of the bait to be used on Miss Emily. Although I suspect that Miss Emily had already made up her mind to humor us, she studiously ignored us as we

twisted dials, and she calmly continued to write in her diary. At last our efforts were rewarded, for we located the broadcast of a recording of London's Big Ben, the bell in the clock tower of the House of Parliament. We turned up the volume. Miss Emily dropped her pen, turned to us, and said in an awe-struck voice, 'Why that is Big Ben! I never thought that I should hear it again!' The set was ours.

With wonder, "Miss Emily" commented in her diary that night that "fearful is the thought that the air is filled with records of all spoken words & sounds." She thought of herself as fortunate to be able to experience and utilize these incredible inventions. Like the automobile, the radio opened to her a world formerly closed to the aged. She could partially transcend the disabilities and limitations to return audially to events and places visited in her earlier years. Furthermore, she could hear speeches, news and commentaries more immediately and less painfully since reading was becoming a demanding task as her eyes continued to weaken.

Writing and reading had been the mainstays and primary pleasures in her life. Now she had to view them as increasingly difficult demands that were to be accomplished despite fatigue, poor muscle control and failing coordination. She preferred the more passive activity of the two, admitting that it was far easier "to let the hours slip by reading." As she approached her one hundredth birthday, she began to relax her demanding self-control and discipline. She most frequently couched life and living in terms of struggle, striving and battles and, even in her nineties, this activist view of life was difficult to abandon. She had to "resist the lure of reading," "summon power to cope with the battle of feeling aged" and had to try "to achieve." Yet for the first time in her life, perhaps, she acknowledged "that a dose of nothingness is good for my joints." She sat in her garden enjoying "the last days of its beautiful life" without feeling guilty for non-achieving. After writing and reading Emily would feel that she "had earned a play spell to browse among my papers." Her mail was filled with impersonal business letters and so she turned to correspondence of another era for personal contact.

This solitary, pleasant, relaxed world was rudely interrupted with a letter from Dr. Frank Graves, Commissioner of Education of New York State inviting her to the Convocation of the University of New

York in October, 1926 where she was to receive an honorary degree of doctor of letters for her work in New York and national education. She would also be the first woman thus honored by the University of the State of New York. Emily, admitting to being "quite thrilled," wrote to Commissioner Graves that "it surely wd be a new sensation to be placed on a pedestal, as it were, a novel experience wh. attracts." She felt she had to refuse, however, since she could not reasonably "venture to make drafts on the future on the hope of added strength lacking but a few weeks of being 99 years old."

Emily's niece Isabel and the teachers of Sherwood Select School would not allow her to refuse so quickly and took great care to see that she was present at the convocation that October. As she was conferred the honorary degree, her friends watched proudly but if Emily were secretly pleased, it is not reflected in her diary entries. She had held a high respect for the teaching profession throughout her life and considered receiving this honor "the lure of my life." But after receiving the degree, she told her diary in her quiet humble way that "I would rather help other people to be spectacular than to be so myself. But I do appreciate the honor which has come to me." She was not consciously self-effacing; rather she had thoroughly incorporated the Quaker tenet of humility—a practice which had played a critical role in governing many of her perceptions and actions during her life. She was frankly bewildered by the outpouring of love and attention that was showered on her in the months after the ceremony. "My friends idealize me to such a degree that I am humiliated by knowing that their estimate is far above the true one." For the past twenty years, her self-image and public identity had not been in apparent conflict. She had viewed herself in positive terms as having successfully worked for and contributed to the community as well as to the status of blacks and women. Her deviance in terms of the marital and social roles she had chosen or advocated was no longer threatening to those around her or painful to her. Many of the unpopular reforms she had favored were now incorporated into state and national legislation. Rather than being labeled deviant, she was credited with having had immense foresight and courage for taking such positions. The honorary degree further aroused this tendency to recognize and praise one of the few survivors of another generation. The degree, or rather the attention and admiration focused on Emily Howland after October, caused her to reassess her self-image in light of this new public image. She found herself falling far short of the mark and candidly wrote "I do not know how I can be to anybody what such tributes imply. I seem so poor to myself."

Once again, her image did not coincide with the popular perspective held of her, but this did not lead to depression or psychological disequilibrium. She had accepted the spatio-temporal limitations her declining physical vitality had placed upon her. Her expectations of self had become more realistic and in proportion to her physical capacities. A change in public image, particularly a highly positive one, would not upset this balance. She was embarrassed by it. She pointed out the discrepancy between her modest view of her life work and the "over much laudation." Finally, she appears to have accepted it as one of those paradoxical mysteries encountered frequently during her many years of living.

Emily, therefore, classified the events surrounding her one hundredth birthday in much the same manner. She dreaded the day for she knew she would be the center of attention and would again be praised. Over one hundred people came to visit her although scores stayed away and visited later that year for fear of overtaxing her strength with too many guests. The day before she had labeled the whole proceedings as "a misfit" but confessed to enjoying it when the day arrived. She gave a copy of Frederick Libby's "What Price Peace" to each guest, feeling that "I have fought for many things in my life—abolition of slavery, education, woman's suffrage, temperance. These victories have been won. Now I hope to see the dawn of uninterrupted international peace."

When the county newspaper carried an editorial and article on her the following day, her only comment was "it was founded on fact, but as all such tributes are too eulogistic I feel the chasm between me and the estimate painful."

Her statement on her activism marks one of the last times that she spoke of reformist concerns in her diary. Her weakness and failing eyesight, with the accompanying difficulty in writing, became more apparent as Emily entered her second century of living. Cornelia Hancock died on December 31, 1926 after a long illness and Emily silently bid her last close friend a touching farewell with this tribute in her diary: "brave & generous, undaunted & kind." She had resigned herself to the fact of death and accepted the com-

𝔈𝔪𝔦𝔩𝔶 𝔥𝔬𝔴𝔩𝔞𝔫𝔡, 𝔏𝔦𝔱𝔱. 𝔇.

November twentieth
Nineteen hundred and twenty-seven

Emily Howland on her 100th birthday, November 20, 1927—a venerated sage. (Courtesy Friends Historical Library of Swarthmore College)

panion fact that now she was even more alone. In February, Emily could no longer stand alone, for, without assistance she would sink to the floor. Her housekeeper, her niece Isabel, and the teachers from the school who boarded at Tanglewild dressed and cared for her. They would type the business letters she dictated, wheel her out to the garden each day and purchase her personal supplies as well as the food for the home. Thanks to these dedicated friends, relatives and employees, Emily's life at Tanglewild continued to run on a smooth, orderly course. By June, both her sight and her hearing had deteriorated so that "my ears report no words over the phone or radio" and "my sight is about one half what it was." Her caustic humor remained as prominent as always. When a group of young students visited her on May Day, she commented that they probably had "never seen anyone so old . . . so (they) filed in & viewed the curiosity. 'Not much of a show' I remarked. This amused PH who burst into spasms of laughter."

The fall and winter of 1928 was spent in trying to maintain a routine of writing and reading without illness but by the new year, her mood of acceptance and passivity had vanished. The burden of lameness, weakness and failing sight made her "long for freedom that my infirmities forbid. I pray for patience." Moreover, the sense of isolation and loneliness was so complete that she experienced a continual longing "for the faces of my old friends." Each month she encountered yet another infirmity signifying both an increased dependency upon her niece Isabel, the teachers and the dormed staff and the coming of her own death. Although loathing this dependency, Emily continued to approach the situation with a healthful blend of humor and patience. When shoes would no longer fit her swollen feet, she jokingly remarked to her housekeeper that her "feet say 'no more shoes forever'."

By early spring she had too little strength for occasional car rides with Mr. Bowen, her chauffeur. Enforced inactivity however reminded her again of her childhood days and youth and made her somewhat "depressed & nervous to a degree hard to control." She could no longer even experience the joy of reading due to blurred vision. She matter-of-factly noted a "strange spell—a sinking I could not speak loud nor use my hands it passed & I was myself again." On June 1, Emily wrote her last entry in her diary. She had become too weak to read and write and therefore decided to dictate her daily diary entries to her housekeeper. She would or could not end the relationship with her oldest friend and confidant, her diary. Each day she would take the elevator from her second floor bedroom to the living room and ride in her wheelchair out to the garden to sit for hours among her beloved flowers. On June 20, Dr. Katie Munhall from Rochester, one of the several younger feminist friends Emily had educated at the Sherwood Select School and later helped through medical school, began writing in Emily's diary at her request. She was no longer able to leave her room and Katie continued to care for her personally. On Wednesday, the 26th of June, she was strong enough to insist that Katie leave her to attend the Old Scholar's Association meeting at the school. When Katie returned one hour later, she was "deeply impressed by the change which had come in that short time—fatigue & utter weariness seemed to have enveloped her like a mantle."

An apathetic state continued through the early evening and by Thursday morning, Emily was too weak to rise. She began to resist however and struggled to remain conscious later that day. When she did lapse into troubled sleep, she had hallucinations of impending danger, such as falling or colliding with an automobile. At other times she had periods of both humor and interest, telling stories from the Civil War and Reconstruction. Friday brought a marked change which was carefully noted by Dr. Munhall: fatigue, no pain and finally, untroubled sleep and peace, evidencing "the closing of the beautiful beneficient life." This condition lasted for almost twenty-four hours. Emily Howland died at 6:50 P.M. on Saturday, June 29, 1929 "with the setting sun casting its radiant color over the world for which she had done so much."

Epilogue

The Howland family cemetery is located on one of the ridges rising above the eastern shore of Lake Cayuga, southeast of the village of Sherwood. A few hundred yards from county roads and bordered by a steep ravine, this quiet spot in the woods now has few visitors. But on the clear warm afternoon of July 2, 1929, a large, yet dignified, group of mourners followed Emily Howland's casket to this spot for burial and stood in silent homage to her memory. The county and state newspapers, as well as the three ministers who led the funeral services, recognized Emily Howland as Cayuga County's most famous, beloved and respected woman. They paid tribute to her long, rich and useful life, recognizing her love of nature, her struggle for the oppressed and her belief in the innate goodness of woman and man. The quality rather than the length of Emily's service to her fellow humans underlie all of these contemporary eulogies. Yet within a few short decades, her name, with few exceptions, was only vaguely remembered as an insignificant or minor figure in key reform movements of the nineteenth and early twentieth century.

Emily Howland's eclipse from public view paralleled the decline in the women's movement during the second quarter of the twentieth century. With the newest activist phase of the women's movement, however, attention is once again being focused on women's lives, roles and contributions. And in the midst of this reawakening Emily Howland stands—a fascinating, paradoxical and complex woman. She was intelligent, humorous, introspective and articulate in detailing her life as an adolescent and as a woman coping with traditional roles, rules and proscriptions for female behavior in nineteenth century America. Although not considered a major historical figure, she does deserve recognition and attention when examining the history of social movements, reforms and humanitarianism in the United States. Yet her unique importance does not lie only in her role of chronicler-participant in the reformist events of over eighty critical years in the life of our nation.

Her most significant historical contribution may ultimately rest in her delineation of a world in which she, as a woman, struggled to lead a satisfying, fulfilling life. Her attempts to realize her potential meant coping, adjusting, redefining and expanding the circumscribed conditions placed upon her by her family and later by her friends and community. At times her struggle was successful; at other times, she failed desperately. A nineteenth century female Odysseus, Emily was shrewd, wise and eloquent in some of these journeys to know herself and those around her better. In other travels though, she was incapable of breaking through her defenses and barriers to reach out to key persons in her life and to realize fully her vast potential. She was both a victim of her times and of her own fears; yet she managed to leave an important legacy to later generations of women. Despite her weaknesses, Emily continued to persevere. She attempted to understand and accept herself as well as the circumstances of her life, to follow faithfully those needs which compelled her to break free from roles imposed on her by herself, her loved ones and society. She wished to spend her life serving others as well as herself, in her own way, at her own pace, and rarely lost sight of this ideal.

Perhaps Emily summarized her odyssey most succinctly and accurately in the epitaph she wrote for her gravestone. In one short sentence she captured her thoughts and behavior as well as those values and beliefs which integrated and made her 101-year inner journey and physical odyssey through life so moving and significant:

EMILY HOWLAND
NOVEMBER 20, 1827
JUNE 29, 1929

———————

SHE WISHED TO HAVE THESE
WORDS UPON HER STONE

———————

I STROVE TO REALIZE MYSELF
AND TO SERVE

Her niece Isabel, speaking perhaps for all those women past and future whose lives Emily touched, added these final words:

PURPOSES NOBLY FULFILLED

———————

Bibliography

Aaron, Daniel (ed). *American in Crisis.* New York: Alfred Knopf, Inc., 1952.

Allsbury, Ruher. *Acts of the Anti-Slavery Apostles.* Concord, New Hampshire: 1880.

Bentley, George F. *A History of the Freedmen's Bureau.* Philadelphia: University of Pennsylvania Press, 1955.

Biographical Review. Leading Citizens of Cayuga County, New York. Boston: Biographical Review Publishing Company, 1894.

Brodie, Fawn M. *Thomas Jefferson: An Intimate History.* New York: W. W. Norton & Company, Inc., 1947.

Chadwick, John (ed). *A Life for Liberty.* New York: Negro University Press, 1969.

Craven, Avery O. *The Repressible Conflict, 1830-1861.* Baton Rouge: Louisiana State University Press, 1939.

Cross, Whitney. *The Burned Over District.* Ithaca: Cornell University Press, 1950.

Curry, Richard O. (ed). *The Abolitionists: Reformers or Fanatics?* New York: Holt, Rinehart and Winston, 1965.

Curti, Merle. *The Growth of American Thought.* New York: 1943.

Davis, Allen. *American Heroine: The Life and Legend of Jane Addams.* New York: Oxford University Press, 1973.

Deutsch, Helene. *Psychology of Women.* New York: 1943.

Dickens, Charles. *Little Dorrit.* London: 1857.

Donald, David: *Lincoln Revisited.* New York: Alfred Knopf, Inc., 1956.

Dumond, Dwight L. *Antislavery: the Crusade for Freedom in America.* Ann Arbor: University of Michigan Press, 1961.

———. *The Anti-Slavery Origins of the Civil War.* Ann Arbor: The University of Michigan Press, 1939.

166 THE WORLD OF EMILY HOWLAND

Elkins, Stanley M. *Slavery: A Problem in American Institutional and Intellectual Life.* Chicago: University of Chicago Press, 1959.

Freud, Sigmund. *Leonardo DiVinci: A Study in Psychosexuality.* New York: Modern Library edition, 1947.

Garrison, Wendell P. *William Lloyd Garrison, 1805–1879.* New York: 1885–1889.

Gordon, Chad and Gergen, Kenneth (eds). *The Self in Social Interaction.* New York: John Wiley & Sons, Inc., 1968.

Hofstadter, Richard. *Anti-intellectualism in American Life.* New York: Alfred Knopf, Inc., 1963.

Kraditor, Aileen S. *Means and Ends in American Abolitionism.* New York: Pantheon Books, 1967.

Kubler-Ross, Elisabeth. *On Death and Dying.* New York: Macmillian and Company, Inc., 1969.

Lane, Ann J. (ed). *The Debate over 'Slavery': Stanley Elkins and His Critics.* Urbana: University of Illinois Press, 1971.

Manschreck, Clyde Leonard. *Melanchthon: The Quiet Reformer.* Abington: 1958.

May, Samuel J. *Some Recollections of Our Anti-Slavery Conflict.* Boston: 1869.

McPherson, Jamesm. *The Struggle for Equality.* Princeton: Princeton University Press, 1964.

Nye, Russell B. *Fettered Freedom: Civil Liberties and the Slavery Controversy, 1830–1860.* East Lansing: Michigan State University Press, 1949.

Peirce, Paul S. *The Freedmen's Bureau, A Chapter of the History of Reconstruction.* Iowa City: State University of Iowa Studies, Volume III. Number 1, 1904.

Perry, Lewis. *Radical Abolitionism: Anarchy and the Government of God in Anti-Slavery Thought.* Ithaca: Cornell University Press, 1973.

Rhodes, James Ford. *History of the United States from the Compromise of 1850.* Volume I. New York: Macmillian and Company, 1906.

Rose, Willie Lee. *Rehearsal for Reconstruction.* New York: The Bobbs-Merrill Company, Inc., 1964.

Shaw, Anna Howard (with collaboration by Elizabeth Jordan). *The Story of a Pioneer.* New York: Harper and Brothers, Inc., 1915.

Sklar, Kathryn Kish. *Catherine Beecher: A Study in American Domesticity.* New Haven: Yale University Press, 1973.

Smith, Page. *Daughters in the Promised Land.* Boston: Little Brown, 1970.

Sorins, Gerald. *Abolitionism: A New Perspective.* New York: Praeger, 1972.

Stampp, Kenneth and Litwack, Leon (eds). *Reconstruction: An Anthology of Revisionist Writings.* Baton Rouge: Louisiana State University Press, 1969.

Stampp, Kenneth. *And the War Came.* Baton Rouge: University of Louisiana Press, 1950.

Storke, Elliot G. *History of Cayuga County, New York.* Syracuse: D. Nason and Company, 1879.

Tager, Jack. *The Intellectual as Urban Reformer.* Cleveland: 1968.
Thomas John L. *The Liberator: A Biography of William Lloyd Garrison.* Boston: 1963.
Tolles, Frederick. *Meeting House and Counting House.* New York: W. W. Norton and Company, 1948.

Manuscripts

Bureau of Refugees, Freedman and Abandoned Lands Records, National Archives, Washington, D.C.
Cornelia Hancock Papers, William C. Clement Library, University of Michigan, Ann Arbor, Michigan.
Elizabeth Cady Stanton Papers, Manuscript Division, Library of Congress, Washington, D. C.
Emily Howland Correspondence, Sophia Smith Collection, Smith College, Northampton, Massachusetts.
Emily Howland Papers, Manuscript Division, John Olin Library, Cornell University, Ithaca, New York.
Garrison Papers, Sophia Smith Collection, Smith College, Northampton, Massachusetts.
Howland Family Papers, Friends Historical Library, Swarthmore, Pennsylvania.
Myrtilla Miner Papers, Manuscript Division, Library of Congress, Washington, D. C.
National American Women Suffrage Association Correspondence, Manuscript Division, Library of Congress, Washington, D. C.
New York Yearly Meeting Records of the Religious Society of Friends, Friends Historical Library, Swarthmore, Pennsylvania.
Phebe King Collection, Howland Family Papers, Friends Historical Library, Swarthmore, Pennsylvania.
Philadelphia Yearly Meeting Records of the Religious Society of Friends, Friends Historical Library, Swarthmore, Pennsylvania.
Private Collection, Emily Howland manuscript material, Phebe M. King, Scipio Center, New York.
Scipio Monthly Meeting Records of the Religious Society of Friends, Friends Historical Library, Swarthmore, Pennsylvania.
War Records Office, Old Military Battles Division, National Archives, Washington, D. C.
William H. Seward Papers, University of Rochester Library, Rochester, New York.
Wister Family Papers, Manuscript Room, Historical Society of Pennsylvania, Philadelphia, Pennsylvania.

Newspapers

Auburn Advertizer-Journal, 1915, 1927–1929.
Auburn Citizen, 1927–1929.
Hamilton Republican, 1941.

Ithaca Journal and Advertiser, 1856-1860.
Liberator, 1843-1853.
National Anti-Slavery Standard, 1850-1865.
New York Spectator, 1856-1859.
New York Times, 1968.
The American Citizen, 1856-1861.

Articles

Brodes, Elaine. "Massachusetts Anti-Slavery Society," *The Journal of Negro History,* XXX, July 1945.
Chapman, Marianna W. "The Position of Women in the Society of Friends" in New York Yearly Meeting pamphlet, 1899.
Coser, Lewis. "Critics of Power: The Abolitionists" in *Men of Ideas.* New York, 1965.
Cudworth, Bessie and Jacobs, Niles (comp): "Emily Howland, 1827-1929, An Unforgettable Person." Private Printing, 1954.
"Excerpts from Justus Allen's Diary, May 20, 1848 to November 4, 1849" in *Yesteryears.* Scipio Center, New York: October, 1957.
Howland Emily. "Early History of Friends in Cayuga County, New York" in *Cayuga County Historical Society Collection Numbers 1 - 2: 1880-1882.* Auburn, N.Y.: Cayuga County Historical Society Publication, 1897.
Judson, Helen. "What Kept Miss Emily Young." Private Printing, 1959.
Keats, John. "There is Something Called Quaker Power" *New York Times Magazine,* March 24, 1968.
"Dedication of the Emily Howland Memorial Library" Private Printing, 1955.
King, Phebe M. "Historical Sketch of the Sherwood Select School, 1871-1964" Private Printing, 1973.
Parkhurst, Genevieve. "A Hundred Years of Living" *Pictorial Review.* September, 1928.
Thomas, John J. "Memoir of David Thomas" in *Cayuga County Historical Collection Number 3-4: 1887-88.* Auburn, N.Y.: Cayuga County Historical Society Publication, 1897.
Wyatt-Brown, Bertram. "Stanley Elkins Slavery: The Anti-Slavery Interpretation Reexamined," *American Quarterly,* Volume XXV, Number 2, May, 1973.
Zorn, Roman J. "The New England Anti-Slavery Society: Pioneer Abolition Reformation," *The Journal of Negro History,* XIII, 1957.

Index

Les Femmes Publishing

EVERYWOMAN'S GUIDE TO COLLEGE
Eileen Gray

The emotional, financial and academic realities of the returning woman student of any age.   903-6, paper, $3.95

TO DELIVER ME OF MY DREAMS
Elizabeth Avakian   •

A present-day journal of the pain and joy of being female.
906-0, paper, $3.95

THE SAME OLD GRIND
Judy Roe

A tragicomic novel about 36 hours in the lives of a bunch of losers in a sleazy burlesque house.   900-1, paper, $4.95

MEANWHILE FARM
Margaret Cheney

A chronicle of the struggles and joys of woman's return to the land.
905-2, paper, $4.95

STAYING MARRIED
Margaret Frings Keyes

A long-overdue examination of *what's right with marriage* by a counselor and therapist.   902-8, paper, $4.95

THE WORLD OF EMILY HOWLAND:
ODYSSEY OF A HUMANITARIAN
Judith Colucci Breault

One of the nineteenth century's foremost but forgotten activists in human rights. (biography)   904-4, paper, $5.95

RUTH KRAMER
Publisher